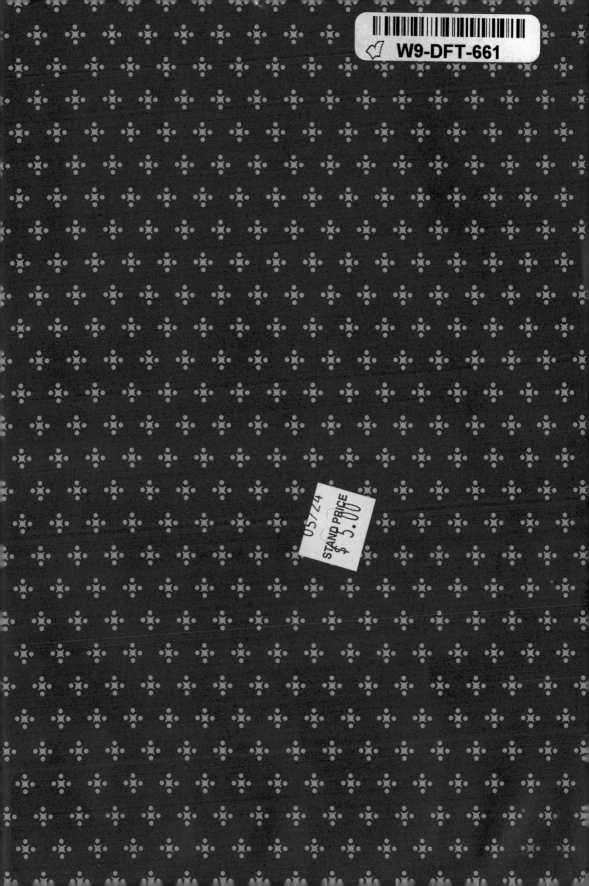

HAPPY HOURS

Bar Stories and Famous Cocktail Recipes

MIRA EITAN

Translator & Editor Karen Marron

Editor for the Hebrew Edition Zohara Ron

Photographer Michal Revivo

Styling Galia Ornan

Designer Studio Keren & Golan

Proofreader Anna O. Aleksandrowicz

Printed by Regent Publishing Services

First Edition in English / January 2019
First Edition in Hebrew / March 2015

LunchBox Press
Publisher and Editor-in-Chief: Ofer Vardi
www.lunch-box.co.il
www.facebook.com / LunchBoxPress
info@lunch-box.co.il

Printed in China 2019
ISBN: 978-1-60280-332-9

HAPPY HOURS

MIRA EITAN

**Bar Stories and Famous
Cocktail Recipes**

TRANSLATED BY KAREN MARRON

LUNCH
BOX

TABLE OF CONTENTS

INTRODUCTION 5

APERITIF

CAMPARI
Something to Start With 11
Americano 14
Negroni 17
Some History: The Origin of
the Word "Cocktail" 18
Bar Stories: Orgasm 23

ANISE

ARAK
Drunk Lit: Ronny Someck 28
From the Hamara to the Club 29
Arak Al-Namroud 30
Arak with Lemon/Grapefruit 34
Bar Stories: In Vino (or in Belgian
Beer) Veritas 36
Some History: Who Invented the
First Pub? 38

VODKA

The Most Popular Drink in the World 44
VODKA STOLICHNAYA 45
Bloody Mary 47
Moscow Mule 48
Drunk Lit: Moscow Petushki 52
Black/White Russian 54
Drunk Lit: Alexander Penn 56
ABSOLUT VODKA 58
Cosmopolitan 60
Vodka Sour 64
Screwdriver 64
KETEL ONE VODKA 66
Vodka Martini 71
Vodka Gibson 72
Bar Stories: Alaska Cocktail 74

GIN

Gin in a Bottle 79
BEEFEATER GIN 85
Singapore Sling 86
Hanky Panky 89
HENDRICK'S GIN 91
Gin & Tonic 94
Gin Basil Smash 97
TANQUERAY GIN 98
Martini Cocktail 100
Fitzgerald 104
Drunk Lit: F. Scott Fitzgerald 107
Bar Stories: Yokhus the Hoarse 108

RUM

Sailors, Slaves and Pirates 113
Havana Club 115
Drunk Lit: Ernest Hemingway 119
Daiquiri 121
Mojito 122
Bar Stories: The Generous Guy 124

TEQUILA

The Blood of the Goddess Mayahuel 128
Margarita 134
Frozen Margarita 137
Tequila Sunrise 138
Some History: The Devil's Brew 139
Bar Stories: What Will the Lady
Be Having? 141

WHISKY

Scotch: Malt or Blended? 144
GLENFIDDICH 147
Whisky Sour 150
Blood and Sand 153
Some History: On Whisky, Taxes
and National Pride 154
CHIVAS REGAL 157

Rob Roy 161
Rusty Nail 162
Distilling the Concepts: A Brief
Glossary of Distillation Terms 164
JOHNNIE WALKER 168
Bar Stories: Johnnie Walker... And
a Lot of It 170
The Chancellor 173
John Collins 174
Some History: Winston Churchill 176
JAMESON 178
The Presbyterian 183
Irish Coffee 184
Bar Stories: The Irish Are Coming 186
AMERICAN WHISKEY 190
What's the Difference Between
Bourbon, Tennessee Whiskey and Rye? 194
Old Fashioned 197
Manhattan 198
Mint Julep 201

COGNAC

The Drink that Was Born by Mistake 204
RÉMY MARTIN 206
What Are Those Letters on the Label? 208
From Gentlemen to Rappers 210
Sidecar 212
Cognac Horse's Neck 215
Some History: Brandy in the Holy Land 216
Drunk Lit: Nathan Alterman 218
Bar Stories: The Wheel Is Come Full Circle 220

DIGESTIF

JÄGERMEISTER
Something to End With 227
Surfer on Acid 230
Jägermeister: A Serving Suggestion 231
Bar Stories: Toothless Mick 234
Bar Stories: Blues for the Boys in Blue 237

DRINKING: A BEGINNER'S GUIDE
The Beginning of a Beautiful Friendship 242

How to Drink: The Rules 243
The Home Bar 245
Equipment 246

⁘

TABLE OF RECIPES

Americano 14
Arak with Lemon/Grapefruit 34
Black/White Russian 54
Blood and Sand 153
Bloody Mary 47
The Chancellor 173
Cognac Horse's Neck 215
Cosmopolitan 60
Daiquiri 121
Fitzgerald 104
Gin and Tonic 94
Gin Basil Smash 97
Hanky Panky 89
Irish Coffee 184
Jägermeister: A Serving Suggestion 231
John Collins 174
Manhattan 198
Margarita/Frozen Margarita 134, 137
Martini Cocktail 100
Mint Julep 201
Mojito 122
Moscow Mule 48
Negroni 17
Old Fashioned 197
The Presbyterian 183
Rob Roy 161
Rusty Nail 162
Screwdriver 64
Sidecar 212
Singapore Sling 86
Surfer on Acid 230
Tequila Sunrise 138
Vodka Gibson 72
Vodka Martini 71
Vodka Sour 64
Whisky Sour 150

INTRODUCTION

About 20 years ago I was a bartender in Israel. I enjoyed working and hanging out behind the bar, and I discovered two interesting facts about that world. The first was that people prefer bars that are dark, because there no one can see all the wrinkles and flaws they think they have. It doesn't matter how old you are; you will always look better in the dark. The second was that at the bar, any bartender who's willing to listen will get to hear some amazing stories.

A bar is an ideal place to find great stories, told without censorship. When people sit around in a dimly-lit room, consuming drinks that unleash their tongues and sometimes also open their hearts, the stories start to pour out all over the place. During my bartending years I wrote down some of the stories that I heard, and I collected some more from bartender colleagues of mine, and put them all together in this book. Some of the anecdotes have appeared previously in print or online, and some are being published here for the first time.

In addition to immersing myself in drinking culture at the bar, I became fascinated by the history of drinking: I loved collecting trivia and facts about alcoholic beverages and specific labels and brands, and discovering the myths and legends behind famous cocktails. I toured breweries, distilleries, and alcohol production plants around the world.

During one of those tours, I arrived at a well-known Cognac house in the Charente region of France. There, a surprise awaited me. Until then I had always assumed that one is supposed to consume Cognac from a stately balloon snifter, while reclining by the fireplace or partaking in an important meeting, while one's hand warms the beverage contained within. The mere mention of ice or any other mixers is frowned upon. But there, at the entrance to the castle, a slender, elderly butler, wearing a three-piece suit with a bowtie, was standing tall and proud, holding a tray of highball glasses, each containing a pale, orange-colored drink.

Those glasses contained none other than a cocktail composed of Cognac, orange juice, and ice. In that moment I let go of all my preconceptions about prestigious drinks and the notion that it is "forbidden" to serve them with ice or to mix them with other beverages. Any drink you have at home can be combined with others, to create all kinds of wonderful beverages, suited to your taste. And this book will help you to do just that: Here you will find recipes, most of them classics, that very wise people created long ago so that we wouldn't have to figure out how to do it ourselves.

This is a personal book, written out of love for the world of alcohol and for the fascinating culture it is built on, for the stories, the legends, and the myths. In writing this, I wasn't trying to cover the entire world of alcohol, and this book is definitely not a comprehensive encyclopedia of alcoholic beverages. This book is a conversation among friends, meant for anyone who has ever sat in a bar or was intrigued by an alcoholic drink at home, for people who want to mix their own classic cocktails, and for those who enjoy salacious stories and historical trivia.

Drinking culture, including the colorful world of cocktails, is part of every aspect of our lives. It is directly connected to the development of culture in general and night life in particular; it inspires technological innovations and the development of specific cuisines; and in many countries it has a key influence on the national economy. Since it first appeared on the scene of human history, alcohol has had an important role in almost every social interaction. And because of alcohol's intoxicating nature—which means it makes us happy and euphoric, and also puts us at ease—many consider it to be a fundamental part of celebrating and having fun. And we deserve to celebrate, too. Cheers!

Mira Eitan

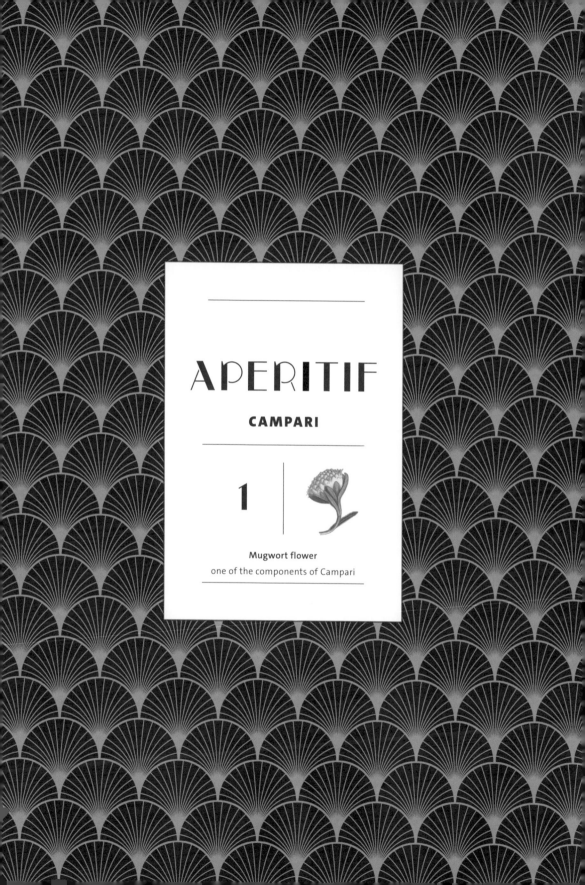

APERITIF

CAMPARI

1

Mugwort flower
one of the components of Campari

SOMETHING TO START WITH

An aperitif is an alcoholic drink that is served before a meal, to whet the appetite. The word "aperitif" is derived from the Latin word *aperire*, which means "to open." Contemporary aperitifs originated in Italy, where people have been drinking them since the 18th century. The basic ingredients of these beverages include grapes, grains, cereals, and other plant-based ingredients, and their alcohol content is usually between 12% and 26%.

Because the aperitif is consumed before a meal, it should not be too sweet, to avoid making the drinker feel full. The herbs, plants, and fruit extracts that it contains are supposed to stimulate the appetite. Its relatively low alcohol concentration prevents it from dulling the taste buds.

The year 1862 marked a major milestone for aperitifs: In that year, Gaspare Campari, a one-time apothecary and later the owner of Caffe Camparino in Milan, created a bittersweet beverage out of a mix of herbs and named it after himself: Campari. Gaspare Campari's invention inspired the custom of drinking bitter beverages before a meal—uprooting the centuries-old tradition of consuming them afterward. Today, Campari is the most popular bitter aperitif in the world, and it is sold in more than 200 countries. It is considered to be the ultimate Italian bitter, no matter how you drink it: mixed with grapefruit juice or with seltzer for beginners, or served neat for die-hard fans.

According to the Campari Group, the company that owns the brand, the bright red beverage is prepared using 86 types of plants, roots, herbs, spices, and fruits. The most prominent among them are ginseng root, citrus peels, and mugwort—which gives the beverage its bitter flavor—in addition to quinine, rhubarb, bergamot oil, and more. The original recipe has not been altered over the years, and it is kept as a family secret. To this day, the mystery is an inseparable part of the magic of the beverage. To prevent the secret formula from being lost, the Campari company makes sure that the people who know the secret never travel together, by train or by plane, in case, God forbid, there is an accident.

The beverage was originally colorless, but over time its manufacturers decided to make it a bright crimson red. Initially, the color was created using carmine dye, produced from cochineal insects that had been dried in the sun and ground into a powder. In the late 1980s, to comply with various health regulations and with Jewish and other dietary laws, the Campari Group began to use only plant-based ingredients in the beverage, and created the red color using pomegranate peels and red food coloring. As of the writing of this book, only three people know the recipe for Campari: Gaspare's great-grandson, the Campari company's master distiller, and the Chief Rabbi of Italy.

Campari's ad campaigns have always been gorgeous and innovative. Their first ad ran in January of 1880, in the most popular daily Italian newspaper at the time, *Corriere della Sera*. In the year 1900, Campari launched its first calendar, which contained portraits of women. Campari's calendars have become an integral part of the brand's tradition. In recent years, the calendars have featured beautiful celebrities dressed in red, including Salma Hayek, Jessica Alba, Mila Jovovich, and Uma Thurman.

In the 1950s the company began to sponsor prestigious sporting events, including the Olympics and Formula 1 races. Later on, they launched a campaign based on colorful cutouts of letters and words. This campaign reached its peak when the Metro system began to operate in Milan in 1964. A large billboard from the campaign is currently on display at the Museum of Modern Art in New York.

BITTER CAMPARI

Campari has a bitter flavor, with a hint of sweetness that's not too cloying, which makes it an excellent prelude to a meal. The drink is not heavy and its alcohol content is not too high (25%), so it also works as a pleasant accompaniment to an afternoon meeting.

Campari can be served in a lowball glass or in a highball glass with ice and seltzer. When mixed with orange juice, grapefruit juice or any other soft drink, it becomes less appropriate as an aperitif because of the high sugar level. Because of Campari's bitter flavor, not everyone enjoys it neat or mixed only with seltzer, so it is often used in cocktails as well.

Americano

The Americano was served for the first time in the 1860s, by Gaspare Campari himself. Initially the cocktail was called the Milano-Torino, named after the birthplaces of its ingredients: Campari, which was from Milan (Milano), and red vermouth, which was from Turin (Torino). At the beginning of the 20th century, bartenders noticed that Americans were particularly fond of the drink and frequently ordered it, and therefore changed its name to "Americano."

The Americano is the first cocktail that James Bond orders in *Casino Royale*, the first book in Ian Fleming's *James Bond* series.

What you need (for one highball glass)	What to do
	Fill the glass with ice.
30 ml Campari	Pour the Campari and the vermouth
30 ml red vermouth	over the ice and add enough seltzer
Seltzer	to reach the rim of the glass.
Ice	Add a stirrer, and garnish with the
Orange or lemon slice for garnish	lemon or orange slice.

Negroni

The Negroni is one of the most famous Campari cocktails, and one of my personal favorites. No one really knows when this cocktail was invented, but according to legend, it was first mixed in Italy in the 1920s and was named after the Italian count Camillo Negroni, who lived in Florence. When visiting his regular bar in Florence, the count would often order the Americano. But the original cocktail wasn't strong enough for him, so he would ask the bartender to substitute a shot of gin for the soda water.

Despite its numerous alcoholic components, this cocktail is pleasant and soft on the palate, probably because of the Campari, which gives the beverage its special qualities.

What you need
(for one lowball glass)

25 ml Campari
25 ml red vermouth
25 ml dry gin
Ice
A twist of orange peel for garnish

What to do

Fill the glass with ice.
Combine all ingredients in a shaker and stir for 20-30 seconds with a spoon.
Strain the cocktail into the glass and garnish with the orange twist.

The Origin of the Word "Cocktail"

Was the original inventor of the cocktail a British officer who entered a bar in 1755 in a poor neighborhood in Madrid? Legend has it that he asked the beautiful barmaid to make him a drink by mixing a few different beverages together. The barmaid poured gin, vodka, orange juice and beer (though it's not clear why), and to mix them all together, she plucked a feather from the tail of a cock that was strutting around the bar. And the officer declared that the drink would be called a cocktail.

Or maybe it was Betsy Flanagan, an innkeeper in New York, who, in 1779, stole roosters from her neighbor to prepare a sumptuous meal for the many French soldiers who visited her pub. She brazenly decorated their drink glasses with the tail feathers of the stolen birds. The soldiers, who enjoyed the meal very much, cheered, *"Vive le cock-tail!"* when they saw the unusual decoration. Another version claims that the name comes from an 18th-century custom in England, in which the winner of a cockfight celebrated the victory by drinking a beverage in which the number of ingredients was equal to the number of feathers that remained in his rooster's tail.

A book called *The Cocktail Book – A Sideboard Manual for Gentlemen*, published in 1933 by John Macqueen, tells yet another story about the origins of the name. During the American Civil War, Squire Allen, the owner of an inn called Bunch of Grapes, who was known for his love of cockfights, discovered that his prize rooster, Jupiter, had been stolen. Allen, heartbroken at the loss, tried to drown his sorrows in drink. He asked Daisy, his favorite barmaid at the inn, to make him a good and refreshing drink that would help him forget his troubles. Daisy filled a glass with ice and mixed i n a few drops of bitters, extracts of roots, wine and some Kentucky whiskey, and decorated the drink with the beautiful feather of a rooster. The innkeeper was very happy with the result, and decided to call the beverage the "cocktail."

And there is a French connection, as well. The French word for an egg cup is *coquetier*. Legend tells that Antoine Peychaude, a Creole apothecary from New Orleans, served his guests a mix of drinks in egg cups, and that this was the source of the name.

Another version, which has no cocks and no tails in it, involves a woman named Coctel, the daughter of the emperor of Mexico. Coctel prepared a drink in honor of a peace treaty that was signed between Mexico and the US in the 1800s.

The first documented case of the word "cocktail" being used to refer to a mix of alcoholic drinks can be traced to a newspaper article published around 1805. The type of beverage described in that article would later come to be known as the Old Fashioned. Credit for coming up with the Old Fashioned cocktail as we know it today is commonly attributed to a bartender at the Pendennis Club in Kentucky, who made the beverage in honor of a famous bourbon distiller named Colonel James E. Pepper. The drink contained a sugar cube with a few drops of bitters and bourbon poured on top, served in a lowball glass (sometimes called an Old Fashioned glass, after the cocktail) with crushed ice and a twist of lemon or orange peel. Colonel Pepper introduced the cocktail to the Waldorf Astoria hotel in New York, where it rose to fame. The author David Embury further consolidated its status when he sang the Old Fashioned's praises in his 1948 book *The Fine Art of Mixing Drinks*.

And indeed, some cocktails have become just as famous as the ingredients they contain. The martini, one of the most popular cocktails of all time, falls into this group. It even has its own glass named after it.

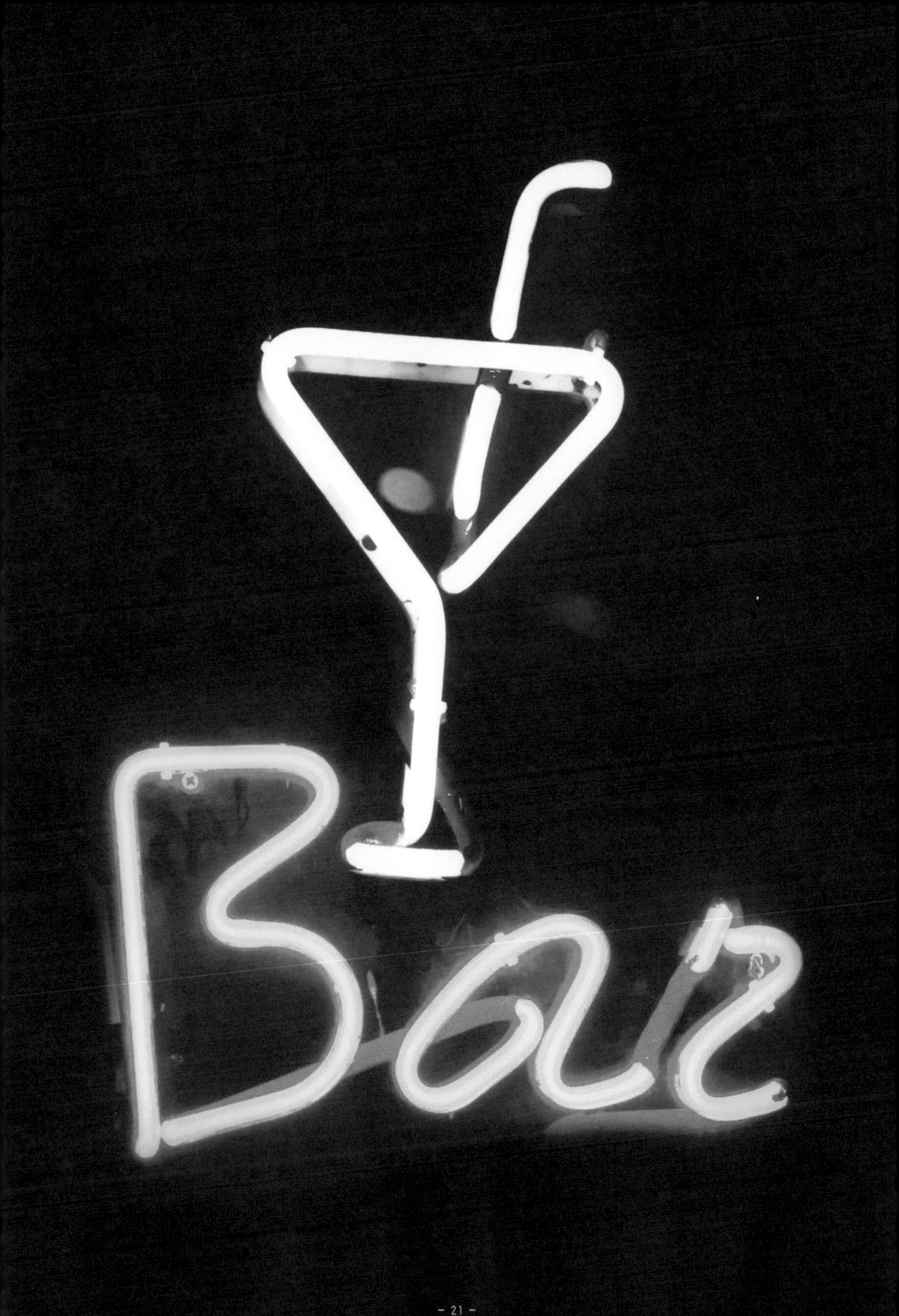
Bar

ORGASM

"It happened many years ago," she told me. "I was young, and new to the world of alcohol, and beer was pretty much the only drink I was familiar with. At the time I was taking a university prep course, and when the course ended, to celebrate, all the students drove down to the Israeli resort town of Eilat for the weekend. In the evening we went to a pub. The music was deafening, but you know, when you're really young, you call that stuff music and even enjoy it, but suddenly when you're older, you're like, 'What's that noise?'

"We all sat in little groups scattered throughout the pub. I ordered my boring drink, beer. I was looking around, and suddenly I noticed that one of my friends was sitting at the bar holding a cocktail glass, sipping a colorful drink that looked like a milkshake. *I didn't know you could drink a milkshake at a pub*, I thought to myself. *Something sweet would be way better than this bitter beer.*

"I got up and made my way towards my friend, fighting the crowds that were mobbing the bar. My friend grinned widely when she saw me. *Too much sugar?* I wondered, and I shouted, 'What's that drink?' 'Or..mmm,' she mumbled to me. I couldn't understand what she was saying; the loud music was pounding in my ears. 'Come again?' I asked. 'What are you drinking?' 'It's a kind of sweet cocktail,' she yelled back, over the music. 'It's called an orgasm.'

"I tasted the drink; it was sweet, smooth and pleasant. Right away I knew that was what I wanted, here and now. 'I want an orgasm,' I said to the busy bartender. 'Whaaaat?' he yelled back. 'Louder, I can't hear you, the music...,' he said, and motioned apologetically towards the massive speakers. 'I WANT AN ORGASM!!' I shouted. At that exact moment, the music stopped. The room was silent. Everyone in the pub had heard my desperate cry. All eyes were on me, and everyone broke into smiles. You have no idea how many guys came up to me that night to volunteer to fulfill my burning needs..."

"There can be nothing more frequent than an occasional drink."

Oscar Wilde

Oscar Wilde

ANISE

ARAK

2

Anise flower
one of the components of arak

Lion's Milk / Ronny Someck

My grandfather was born in the lands of arak
and the bottles had labels with drawings of lions,
manes combed, posing as sheep.
"This is the King of beasts,"
his finger would tremble
and the wind mapped in his thin mustache
parallels of latitude
and meridians of longitude,
the jungle of my dreams.
It's a good thing I lost my way,
otherwise Jack Daniels could have been my dad
and gin would be rocking
the tonic cradle in my throat.

And it's only into the empty bottles
I wanted to throw out to sea
that I've slipped a note in his memory
drunk with love.

Translated from the Hebrew by Vivian Eden.
The Hebrew version of "Lion's Milk"
appears in Someck's collection *Gan Eden Le-Orez*
[Paradise for Rice], Zmora-Bitan, 1996.

FROM THE HAMARA TO THE CLUB

Ah, anise. Either you love it or you hate it, but you can't be indifferent to it. The Mediterranean Basin is the birthplace of anise drinks: Ouzo comes from Greece, raki comes from Turkey, pastis and Pernod come from France, sambuca is from Italy, and arak hails from the Middle East, namely, Lebanon and Jordan. Arak is also the anise drink of choice in Israel, my home country—and in recent years, perhaps surprisingly, it has become a hot trend in the bar scene.

Arak used to be associated with old men playing backgammon in *hamaras*—an ancient type of Middle Eastern dive bar, filled with smoke—or praying at the synagogue. But in recent years, young Israeli clubbers have discovered the traditional beverage, and have started ordering it like there's no tomorrow. Maybe it's because of its down-to-earth price, which is appropriate for the current economic climate. Or maybe people have finally internalized the fact that we live in the Middle East, and in the heat of the summer it makes more sense to drink arak than to drink whisky.

The world's undisputed capital of arak production is Zahlé in Lebanon, the capital of the Beqaa Governorate, which is known for its vineyards. The name arak comes from the Arabic word for "sweat", and it refers to the distillation process, which involves evaporation and condensation. The original beverage is made mostly of grapes, which go through a process of fermentation and distillation. The liquid is dripped on top of natural anise seeds, and their flavor soaks into the alcohol. Arak is also referred to as *halib al sba*, or "lion's milk." "Lion" because it is considered to be a strong, manly drink, which makes the drinker feel like a lion, and "milk" because when water is added to arak its color changes from clear to milky white.

ARAK AL-NAMROUD

The story of Arak al-Namroud, a prominent brand of arak in Israel, begins with Elias Karem, a former member of the South Lebanon Army (SLA). The SLA and Israel were allies in a 15-year conflict with Hezbollah in South Lebanon. In 2000, the Israeli army unilaterally withdrew its troops from South Lebanon, and many SLA members—including Elias—fled to Israel. Elias worked as a school principal in the city of Nahariya, teaching children of other SLA families. At the same time, he was looking for a way to do something special that would bring Lebanon to Israel, something that would strengthen his ties to the new country and to his former homeland. Lebanon is known for its arak, and Elias, a descendant of generations of arak distillers, got some of his SLA friends together and started working on his life's mission. In 2003, the Arak al-Namroud distillery opened in the Goren Industrial Park, located in the Western Galilee.

Elias produces arak according to Lebanese methods that have been passed down for generations, while following the guidelines of Israel's Ministry of Health and requirements of Jewish dietary law. Galilee arak is special in that is made only with natural ingredients, and the alcohol is distilled from scratch, and is not produced synthetically using chemicals. Because of Elias, in a short time, Zahlawi-style arak transformed from a secret known only to a select few into a massive success story.

Elias's arak is distilled in traditional copper stills, similarly to Cognac. After an initial round of distillation, in which alcohol is produced from white grapes, exquisite Syrian anise seeds are added, and the alcohol is distilled two more times. Arak al-Namroud has a smooth and velvety texture; it is aromatic with a hint of sweetness, and an intoxicating flavor of anise.

"It takes only one drink
to get me drunk.
The trouble is, I can't
remember if it's the
thirteenth or the
fourteenth."

George Burns, American
comedian and entertainer

Arak has medicinal qualities. "Arak is good for your health," its acolytes claim, "especially when it's made exclusively out of natural ingredients." It helps with digestion, problems with blood vessels, and the heart; it makes headaches disappear, kills germs, and also helps with a sore throat or toothache. And most importantly — "It's an excellent balm for the soul."

Arak al-Namroud has a smooth and velvety texture and is soft and thick on the palate; it is aromatic with a hint of sweetness, and an intoxicating flavor of anise.

Anise

How do people drink arak in its country of origin, Lebanon? Because arak's alcohol content is relatively high (50%), it is customary to pour it into a relatively narrow glass, up to a third of the glass's height, and only then add equal parts water and ice. It is important to add the arak, water, and ice in that order, to obtain a consistent milky texture. If you start with the water or ice and only then add the arak, you will get uneven white threads in the glass. When you finish drinking, check the white residue that is left on the glass. The milkier its texture, the higher the quality of the arak.

Arak with Lemon/Grapefruit

Arak is a refreshing summer drink and pairs beautifully with meat, fish, salads and any Mediterranean dish. The best-known arak cocktail in Israel, and the one that makes arak attractive even to people who don't love anise, is arak with lemon and mint. A refreshing drink for hot summer days, it doesn't get more Mediterranean than this.

**What you need
(for one highball glass)**

60 ml arak
Fresh lemonade or fresh-squeezed grapefruit juice
Ice
Fresh mint leaves for garnish

What to do

Pour the arak into a glass with ice. Add the lemonade or grapefruit juice up to the rim of the glass. Garnish with mint leaves.

IN VINO (OR IN BELGIAN BEER) VERITAS

Even a novice waiter can tell you that a successful blind date will always end in a very large tip. The person who's paying for the meal will try to make an impression on his/her date and won't spare any expense in showing gratitude to his hosts. And that night, the good-looking girl who'd just entered the pub alone looked like a promising half of a blind date: She chose a table for two and sat down facing the door. The waitress gave her a menu. "I'm waiting for someone," said the good-looking girl. So we waited.

We hadn't been waiting long when a tall man appeared in the doorway. He was wearing a brown jacket, and his eyes scanned the tables methodically. They locked onto the girl who was sitting alone. He walked up to her confidently and introduced himself. The waitress smiled: We had a blind date. The two of them began to study their menus to get through the first few minutes of awkward silence.

The waitress came back to them to take their order. The order was the usual fare for first dates: not too much food (so you don't come across as greedy), no hard alcohol (so you don't come off as a drunk), and delivered in a way that makes you seem like you know what you're talking about. She ordered a Campari and soda, and he ordered a Belgian beer. The beer arrived in a nice glass that immediately attracted his attention, because it was decorated with the beautiful logo of the famous brewery. "Can I have the glass?" he asked. "I don't have one like this in my collection."

Even though any novice waiter can tell you that there is nothing more important than making sure that a blind date goes well, the long-legged waitress answered: "I'll ask the bartender and get back to you in a minute." And then she turned the request over to me. I had to say no, despite my enormous empathy for people on blind dates. That type of beer had only recently arrived in the country. We'd just started carrying it that week, and it had arrived with a small set of only six glasses. I asked the waitress to apologize and explain the situation as politely as possible.

"Unacceptable," was the surprising response. Maybe he was trying to come across as assertive to the girl sitting across from him. "Tell the bartender to think about it again. I really want this glass." When they got up at the end of the evening, they indeed left behind a generous tip, as would be expected from someone who had an enjoyable first date. But they also left behind a table with no glasses on it—to the waitress's dismay.

Two weeks later, at the same time, the couple reappeared. Making themselves at home, they sauntered over to the same table. The long-legged waitress and I exchanged glances. It was clear to both of us that we had identified the perpetrators. They placed the exact same order: Campari and soda and Belgian beer. This time, we took revenge. The prestigious imported beer was served in a simple local glass. "I want the original glass," said the man in his familiar assertive tone. "Sorry, all the glasses we have are in use," Long-Legs answered. He looked around: It was still early; the place was almost empty. It didn't look like there was a shortage of glasses. He didn't take the hint: "Can't you find one glass for me?" "No, we have a problem with those glasses," the waitress explained, looking him right in the eye. "They're too nice, and people just steal them from the bar. That's why we don't have enough glasses for our customers." This time the tip was a lot smaller.

WHO INVENTED THE PUB?
AND WHO WAS THE FIRST BARTENDER?

The pub is not a modern invention. Its origins go back to the ancient cultures of Mesopotamia, Canaan, and Phoenicia, in which it was customary to hold banquets in the family burial cave, alongside the bones and skulls of the family ancestors. These feasts were held during periods of mourning and on other occasions—particularly when trouble hit the village. Participants would serve their dead ancestors beverages and food such as milk, beer, lamb and beef, to appease them and ask them to put a good word in with the gods. This ritual is referred to in the Old Testament, in the book of Jeremiah: "For thus says the Lord, Do not enter a house of mourning [banqueting], or go to lament or to console them; for I have withdrawn My peace from this people" (16:5; New American Standard Bible). As the quote suggests, this custom was frowned upon in ancient Hebrew society, probably because it honored other gods, and Jewish priests were not allowed near it. But the biblical Hebrew word for the ritual, *marze'akh*, survived, and is the basis for the modern Hebrew word for "pub": *beit marze'akh*, which means a house of drinking and debauchery.

Judaism is not opposed to alcohol per se, quite the opposite. Almost every holiday involves drinking ceremonial wine, and during the Purim holiday people are explicitly required to drink "until they cannot tell the difference between the cursed Haman and the blessed Mordechai," as it says in the Talmud. The ancient Hebrews used to drink wine in religious ceremonies and at times of celebration. Wine and "strong drink" are mentioned in the Bible hundreds of times, usually with positive connotations, as something that "cheers Gods and men" (Book of Judges, 9:13, NASB). Countless archeological artifacts discovered in Israel bear witness to the role of wine in ancient Jewish culture, including thousands of wine presses and ceramic jugs with dregs of alcoholic drinks. Even Hasidic Jews give wine and drink a place of honor, as part of the belief that life on Earth is a vessel for worshipping God and for attaining spiritual elevation, through eating, drinking, manual labor, and storytelling.

Wine even has its own special blessing in Jewish tradition: *Borei pri ha-gafen;* "Blessed be the fruit of the vine." According to one of the opinions in the Talmud, the Tree of Knowledge was actually a grapevine, hinting at the devastating potential of drinking wine. Noah is the first drunk person—and the first winemaker—explicitly mentioned in the Bible: "Then Noah began farming and planted a vineyard. He drank of the wine and became drunk" (Genesis 9:20-21). Another famous case of drunkenness in the Bible is the story of Lot, Abraham's nephew, who escaped the city of Sodom with his family. His daughters, thinking that the world, like Sodom, would soon be destroyed, got him drunk and then had sex with him, trying to get pregnant. That story is the origin of the Hebrew expression "drunk as Lot," which refers to the drunkest you can possibly be, when you are completely unaware of what you're doing.

The first bartender in the Bible was Pharaoh's chief cupbearer, who would pour drinks for his king. One day, the cupbearer infuriated the Pharaoh when he served him a drink with a fly inside it. He had to temporarily relocate his bar to jail, until he was forgiven and reinstated to his original

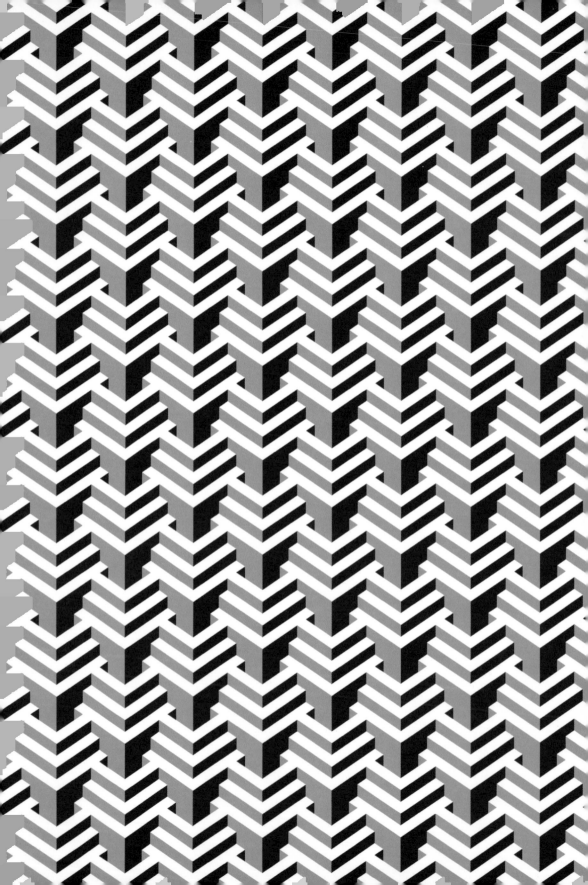

VODKA

3 |

A grain of wheat
one of the components of vodka

"A holiday without vodka is like a sailor without a ship."

Russian proverb

THE MOST POPULAR DRINK IN THE WORLD

Vodka is the most popular alcoholic drink in the world. Theoretically, the beverage has no smell, taste, or color, and yet it seems like a new brand of vodka is launched every day, with its producers willing to swear that their vodka is different from all the others, better, tastier, more pleasing to the palate. The word "vodka" comes from Slavic languages, and it means "little water", both in Russian and in Polish. Vodka started to be produced commercially in Russia and in Poland in the 16th century, but its popularity really began to take off in the 19th century. Around 1975, vodka sales skyrocketed all over the world and surpassed those of any other alcoholic beverage.

The debate about who produced vodka first, Poland or Russia, will probably continue forever, but one fact is indisputable: Russia is the world's unofficial capital of vodka production. Russians have been drinking a great deal of alcohol since the Middle Ages, before the advent of vodka, but vodka was the first alcoholic beverage to be sold on the Russian market, and everyone drank it. The authorities, recognizing the drink's economic potential, nationalized the production of vodka to earn money off the taxes that they could charge and created giant monopolies. For 400 years, the state had exclusive authority to distill vodka, and vodka has played an important role in Russia's economy and culture ever since.

Tsar Ivan IV, who ruled Russia during the years 1547–1584, and was perhaps better known by his nickname, "Ivan the Terrible", was the first Russian monarch to open a *kabak* (pub) in the country. He was responsible for establishing hundreds of pubs throughout Russia, ensuring a rapid flow of funds to the palace. In 1930 in the Soviet Union, stores selling vodka outnumbered stores selling meat, vegetables or fruit, and every soldier received vodka as part of his daily rations. In short, vodka was an inseparable part of life. In the mid-20th century, alcohol consumption in the Soviet Union was so high that 20% of the population were considered alcoholics. In 1992, after the fall of Communism, Boris Yeltsin eliminated the monopolistic laws that the government had imposed on vodka production and opened up the market so that anyone who wanted to could manufacture the beverage. Today, more than 1,500 brands of vodka are produced in Russia alone, and it looks like that number will only continue to grow.

VODKA STOLICHNAYA

When you say "Russian vodka", one of the first names that comes to mind is Stolichnaya, the country's best-known and best-selling vodka brand. The word is a form of the word "столица" (pronounced *STOO-lee-tza*), which means "capital city" in Russian. The name was chosen to create a sense of pride among the Russian people and encourage them to drink as much as possible. Stolichnaya, also known by the nickname "Stoli", was produced for the first time by Viktor Svirida, a senior distiller in the Liviz distillery in St. Petersburg. The distillery, which was founded in 1897, produced many different brands of vodka, but Svirida created a vodka that was different from its predecessors. It was made exclusively from wheat, and unlike other vodka brands, it was filtered through quartz rather than through charcoal, which made the resulting spirit almost perfectly clear, and made the vodka smoother. In 1972, the Soviet authorities decided that Stoli, the definitive traditional Russian vodka, was the only Russian brand that would be sold outside the country. That decision held until the 1980s, so for years, Stolichnaya was almost the only Russian vodka that the Western world was familiar with.

Portrait of Queen Mary I of England. Painting by Antonis Mor, 1554

Vodka is usually consumed neat, on the rocks, or straight from the freezer in a shot glass or chaser; in the latter case, its texture is smooth and oily, making it easy to drink. Vodka is also very popular as a cocktail ingredient: Because it is neutral and has no color, taste or smell, it doesn't influence the flavor of a cocktail—it just makes it stronger. Stolichnaya comes in many different flavors—citrus, strawberry, cranberry, peach, orange, vanilla, coffee, and others, each of which can add a unique, interesting twist to a cocktail.

Bloody Mary

The Bloody Mary is one of the most classic cocktails, and you can drink it at just about any time, on its own or with a meal. There are debates as to the origins of the cocktail. The French claim it was invented in Paris (at a bar that Ernest Hemingway used to frequent), whereas the Americans claim that it was first produced at the St. Regis Hotel in New York. There, for the first time, someone had the idea of enhancing the basic combination of vodka and tomato juice by adding salt, black pepper, Worcestershire sauce, Tabasco sauce, lemon juice, and crushed ice. Little by little the drink became known as the "Bloody Mary", probably because of its red color, similar to the color of blood. In the 1960s it became popular to serve the cocktail with a celery stalk, a practice inspired by the special request of a guest at the Ambassador Hotel in Chicago.

The identity of the "Mary" in the cocktail's name is also up for debate. One popular assumption is that the name refers to Mary I, who was the Queen of England in the mid-16th century and a Roman Catholic, and was called "bloody" because she persecuted Protestants and killed hundreds of them for their faith. Another, somewhat questionable version claims that the name refers to a queen who got advice from a witch, who told her to bathe in a tub full of virgins' blood. A more current suggestion is that the cocktail was named after Mary Pickford, a star from the early days of cinema, who was known for her love of drinking.

What you need
(for one highball glass)

60 ml vodka
120 ml tomato juice
10 ml lemon or lime juice
¼ tsp minced white horseradish
   (or to taste)
4 drops of Tabasco sauce
Worcestershire sauce
Salt
Pepper

Ice
A celery stalk and a lemon slice
for garnish

What to do

Fill the glass with ice. Pour in
liquids, add horseradish and
seasoning. The drink can be
shaken beforehand or stirred in
the glass. Garnish with the celery
stalk and lemon slice.

Moscow Mule

The Moscow Mule was actually invented in the US, around 1940. The owner
of a Hollywood bar was trying to help a vodka manufacturer promote his
product, while at the same time promoting his own homemade ginger beer.
He mixed the two together, and the Moscow Mule was born. This cocktail
started the vodka frenzy in the US during the 1950s. The classic way of serving
it is in a copper mug. The cocktail is summery and fresh, and has recently
become trendy once again, as ginger beer is experiencing a resurgence.

What you need
(for one highball glass)

60 ml vodka
20 ml fresh-squeezed lime juice
Ginger beer or ginger ale
Ice
Mint leaves and a slice of lime
for garnish

What to do

Fill the glass with ice. Pour vodka and
lime juice into the glass. Add ginger
beer/ale up to the rim of the glass.
Garnish with mint leaves and lime.

**Some people also add a piece
of ginger root.**

Moscow Mule (see p. 48)

Moscow-Petushki (published in English under several different titles, including *Moscow to the End of the Line*, *Moscow Stations*, and *Moscow Circles*) is the title of a wonderful book written by Venedikt Yerofeyev, an alcoholic. The book, which is the best known of Yerofeyev's works, is a monologue that unfolds over several hours of travel on a train from Moscow to the narrator's hometown of Petushki, only 120 kilometers away. The monologue is packed with memories and political and social criticism (as a result of which the book was banned in the Soviet Union and was subsequently photocopied and distributed as contraband, turning it into a cult classic). And of course, it's overflowing with alcohol. Among other things, the narrator offers several impossible cocktail recipes. For example, a cocktail called The Tear of a Komsomol Girl (the Komsomol was a Communist youth movement) includes lemonade, verbena and lavender, "Forest Water" eau de cologne, nail polish, and mouthwash.

As might be expected from a Russian book, vodka has a place of honor. In the words of the narrator: "Somebody drinking vodka neat will either keep a clear head and a sound memory, or, on the contrary, lose both of them. But as far as the Tear of a Komsomol Girl goes, it's quite funny: You can drink 100 grammes of the Tear, and your memory's sound as a bell, but it's as if you've no head at all. You drink another 100 grammes and you surprise yourself: Where did I get this fantastic clear head? And where the hell's my memory gone? Even the recipe for the Tear is strong stuff. And once the cocktail's mixed, a mere whiff of it can cause a momentary loss of sensation and consciousness. It did with me, anyway."

From *Moscow Stations*, Faber & Faber, 1997, translated by Stephen Mulrine

Black/White Russian

The Black Russian cocktail got its name because its main ingredient is vodka, which is identified with Russia, and the vodka is mixed with coffee liqueur, which makes it turn black. The cocktail's white counterpart also includes cream, which gives it its white color. The White Russian was named after the soldiers of the White Army, which operated against the Bolsheviks during the Russian Civil War; the members of that army were called "White Russians" to distinguish them from the "Reds", the Communists.

It's not clear which of the two beverages was invented first. The first documented use of the expression "White Russian" as the name of a cocktail was in a newspaper in California on November 21, 1965. In the late 1990s the cocktail enjoyed a surge in popularity thanks to the cult film *The Big Lebowski*, in which Jeffrey Lebowski, "The Dude", drinks the beverage several times.

What you need
(for one lowball glass)

40 ml vodka
20 ml coffee liqueur
20 ml cream
   (only for the white version)
Ice

What to do

Fill the glass with ice.
Pour in ingredients and stir gently with a stirrer.

Alexander Penn (1906–1972) was one of the most—perhaps the most—lyrical and flamboyant poets in Israel: handsome, bohemian, a drinker, a partier, a boxer, a painter, a filmmaker, and a serial lover. He was married twice and fathered three girls and a boy, with three different women. The myth and the legends have become intertwined with his real life, to the point where even his official biographies have found it challenging to separate fact from fiction.

According to Penn's stories, his father's side of the family was descended from the rabbis of Chabad, whereas his maternal grandfather, named Jensen, was a Swedish count, an oceanographer, a bear hunter, and a fisherman. Alexander's mother had died when he was a baby, and Jensen raised him until the age of 10 in a secluded igloo in Siberia on the shores of the Arctic ocean. After his grandfather was eaten by a polar bear (Penn claims), Alexander was left alone on the tundra and traveled more than 6,000 kilometers over several years, during the Russian Civil War, partly on his own and partly in the company of street urchins, until he found his Jewish father, who was living at the time in the North Caucasus. According to an alternative version, Penn was born in the Ukraine to Jewish parents. So to quote one of Penn's most famous poems: "Did it happen? Or not?"

His love of drinking features in many of his classic poems.

Fly away / Alexander Penn

Fly, fly away
Gloom, pensiveness, dolor
Stay, life, stay
Grog bring, and my amour...

Salud, my darling, little sister of mine
A wave will sweep me away tomorrow,
Lord knows where or why...

Waves, waves, I am adrift at sea.
Line, twine, aboard my roiling boat.
Darlings at both ports await me
One's a maiden, aye,
the other's a harlot.

Grog, grog I will drink today
The fish will have me on the morrow.
Damn, damn it all! Today is still today
Bring food, man, and grog to drown
my sorrow!

Translated from the Hebrew by Oded Even-Or

Alexander Penn at Café Kassit in Tel Aviv, 1965.
From the Alexander Penn Archives, Kipp Center, Tel Aviv University.

ABSOLUT VODKA

Sweden has a massive vodka industry. As early as the 15th century there were dozens of vodka distilleries in Sweden, and within 100 years there were hundreds. Whereas in Eastern Europe vodka was distilled from potatoes and rye, Swedish vodka was made from wheat only. Absolut Vodka was first produced in Sweden in 1879, but it truly rose to fame only a century later. Lars Olsson Smith was the man behind Absolut. He was the first Swedish vodka manufacturer to use the method of continuous distillation, instead of the traditional batch distillation method, which uses pot stills. The continuous distillation method produced a spirit that was smooth, pure, and flavor-free—much more so than any other vodka brand in Sweden. Smith named his vodka Absolut Rent Brännvin, the absolutely pure spirit. Vodka immediately became a hit among the Swedish people, and Smith was called Sweden's "Vodka King."

Smith was also a marketing genius, and his original, innovative marketing campaigns turned his vodka into an international phenomenon. In the 1970s Absolut began to be marketed in the US, after some adjustments were made to the brand. Specifically, the bottle was made to look like an old-style medicine bottle, to make Americans associate it with health. And the name of the vodka was shortened to Absolut Vodka. After a brilliant mass marketing campaign, in 1985 Absolut became the highest-sold imported vodka in the US. Today Absolut is the second-best-selling vodka brand in the world.

Over the years, Absolut has used art as a marketing tool. Diverse artists working in many different genres and media—including painters, musicians, fashion designers, and filmmakers—were recruited to bolster the brand's image as something fashionable, popular and high-quality. Andy Warhol,

Lars Olsson Smith

Keith Haring, Jean-Michel Basquiat, Louise Bourgeois, and Spike Lee are just a few of the famous names on Absolut's roster. Pretty much everyone is familiar with Absolut's ads and posters, even people who've never tasted vodka, and these ads are responsible for turning Absolut into such a well-known brand.

Vodka-based cocktails are usually fairly simple. For example, it doesn't get much more basic than the Absolut Red Bull, one of the most famous Absolut cocktails. But I'm not about to print that recipe. I'd rather focus on finer things.

Cosmopolitan

The Cosmopolitan cocktail, or the Cosmo, is easy to make, and it has become one of the most popular cocktails of all time. It owes its fame to the popular TV series *Sex and the City*, where it appeared dozens of times. The Cosmo is an excellent example of how well vodka mixes with fruit juice. In fact, the cocktail was apparently invented as part of an advertising campaign for Ocean Spray juice, back in the 1960s.

What you need
(for one cocktail glass)

40 ml vodka
20 ml orange liqueur
20 ml fresh-squeezed lime juice
40 ml cranberry juice
Ice
Lemon/orange wedge for garnish

What to do

Fill the glass with ice.
Shake up all the ingredients in a shaker with ice.
Take the ice out of the glass and strain the cocktail into it.
Garnish with a lemon or orange wedge.

Vodka sour (see p. 64)

Vodka Sour

The vodka sour belongs to the family of sour drinks: cocktails that are a little bit sweet and a little bit sour, and served with a lot of ice. They're refreshing and light, very popular, and easy to make.

**What you need
(for one lowball glass)**

60 ml vodka
30 ml sour: lemon juice and sugar
    syrup, at a ratio of 3 parts lemon
    to 1 part syrup.
A little bit of lime juice
Ice
A slice of lemon for garnish

What to do

Fill the glass with ice.
Shake up all the ingredients
in a shaker with ice and pour
into the glass.
Add a stirrer and garnish with
the lemon wedge.

Screwdriver

Vitamin C, anyone? This orange-juiced-based cocktail is one of the easiest drinks to make. It's refreshing and fruity, and yet another example of the power of vodka in cocktails. Because it contains squeezed orange juice, this cocktail is also great with brunch. You can swap out the orange juice for cranberry or grapefruit juice, but then you can't call it a screwdriver.

**What you need
(for one highball glass)**

60 ml vodka
Fresh-squeezed orange juice
Ice
Orange wedge for garnish

What to do

Fill the glass with ice.
Pour vodka into the glass.
Add orange juice up to the rim
of the glass. Stir well and garnish
with the orange wedge.

KETEL ONE VODKA

Though vodka is a Polish or Russian invention, the ultra-premium vodka brands don't necessarily come from Eastern Europe. Some are made in countries that aren't typically associated with vodka. There are no hard and fast rules that determine whether a particular vodka brand is premium or ultra-premium, but the basic idea is that these vodkas are higher quality than regular vodka. And what makes the difference? Any number of things: ingredients; a large number of continuous distillations; a large number of filtrations through active charcoal; the use of a combination of batch distillation and continuous distillation; or the use of batch distillation only. The combination of all these elements, or even just a few of them, elevates the vodka's flavor—or, more precisely, its lack of flavor.

The prices of ultra-premium vodka brands are similar to those of premium brands of whisky, and their bottles are usually eye-catching, designed to convey luxury. Ketel One is one such ultra-premium vodka brand, produced in the Netherlands for more than 300 years by the Nolet family. The Nolet distillery was founded by Joannes Nolet in 1691, in the city of Schiedam in the Netherlands. Nolet's goal was to produce jenever, a beverage that started as a treatment for stomach and kidney pains and that eventually developed into what is now called gin.

According to Nolet family legend, a family member discovered an old recipe for an alcoholic beverage in the family vault. After some trial and error and adjustments to the recipe, he finally reached a product he was happy with and ultimately produced... vodka, which was smooth, pure, and delicate. He named the product "Ketel One", after the oldest copper still in the distillery, which was called Distilleerketel #1 (distillation kettle 1) and had been in operation since 1864.

The Nolets' distillation process is a closely-guarded secret, which has been passed down from father to son for ten generations. Even the shape of the bottle is part of the family tradition: It is the same as the shape of the bottle used for the first spirit that the Nolet distillery produced. Over the years, the family has prioritized one thing over all else: superior product quality. In the 1990s the Nolets began to market their vodka outside the Netherlands, mainly in the US. The family's marketing approach was somewhat unusual: Representatives of the family loaded crates of bottles of their vodka and drove off to conquer America. At first they went from bar to bar to pitch their product, and very quickly the rumors about the high-quality vodka began to spread, and the orders started flowing in.

Around that time, the Nolet family established a distillery in the US. In the year 2000 the distillery produced the first ultra-premium citrus-flavored vodka, flavored with natural citrus fruits. The company's products are currently sold all over the world.

Distilleerketel #1, from the label on the bottle

Schiedam, the Netherlands, 1880

Vodka is a key player in the cocktail scene, and a new high-quality vodka brand is introduced into the market almost once a month. Even though the cocktail world has been getting richer over the past decades, offering enormous variety, the classics never go out of style, and every self-respecting bar should be able to make them.

Vodka Martini

Though the classic martini cocktail—probably the most famous cocktail in the world—is based on gin, it has a respectable vodka-based alternative. This cocktail came into being in the 1950s, when the Americans discovered vodka, and it was called a "Kangaroo." Bartenders created this cocktail for people who preferred to avoid the spicy flavors and aromas of gin and wanted something simpler and cleaner.

Ian Fleming's James Bond—a.k.a. Secret Agent 007—is known for ordering a vodka martini, emphasizing that it should be "shaken, not stirred."

What you need (for one martini glass)	What to do
60 ml vodka	Stir the ingredients with a long bar spoon in a shaker with ice. Pour into the glass and garnish with the green olive on a toothpick.
15 ml dry white vermouth	
Ice	
Green olive on a toothpick for garnish	

The less vermouth you put in, the drier the cocktail will be. If you want to channel 007, shake the shaker—don't stir.

Vodka Gibson

The Gibson is another type of martini cocktail. The original cocktail was, of course, based on gin, and that's how Winston Churchill liked to drink it—which he did often. The Gibson is also featured on the TV show *Mad Men*, where it is the preferred beverage of Roger Sterling, a partner at the Sterling Cooper advertising agency. Here is the vodka version of the Gibson.

What you need
(for one martini glass)

60 ml vodka
15 ml dry white vermouth
Ice
Cocktail onion for garnish

What to do

Put the ingredients in a shaker with ice and stir with a long bar spoon.
Pour into a glass and drop the onion inside.

The less vermouth you put in, the drier the cocktail will be.

ALASKA COCKTAIL

"Follow me!" the commander roared and, with his five soldiers, invaded the bar. The boys obeyed; they were willing to follow their leader through fire and water, and they all sat down in a row in front of me at the bar. Many pairs of eyes turned to stare at the group. We didn't get many soldiers in uniform at our pub. The commander asked my name and immediately started shouting orders at me, too: "Mira, we're thirsty! How much longer are we going to have to wait?"

Orders were taken, the taps—and bottles—were opened, and the men started drinking. Round after round and then another round. Three hours went by, with the commander's voice thundering over the music in the background. The leader knew what he wanted to drink, but his young subordinates left their lives in my hands: "Whatever you decide. Mix up something good." It was obvious that they weren't used to drinking, but their leader had decided that tonight they would drink, and now was not the time to refuse an order. They tried to pace themselves, but they were unsuccessful under the commander's watchful eye.

After he had gotten his five soldiers, and himself, good and drunk, the commander ordered another round. Barely conscious, one of the soldiers signaled that they'd all had enough and should probably stop drinking. But good luck getting out of a direct order—or, even worse, trying to reason with a drunk commander. As I was about to pour the next round I got some plaintive looks from the guys, begging me not to give them any more alcohol. But I, too, feared the commander, who looked like he was going to yell at me again.

I rushed to pour him another drink, and next to it I arranged five glasses full of ice water, a lemon, and stirrers for the boys, who thanked me with their drooping eyelids. "What is this?!" roared the commander, as I served the lemon-garnished highballs to his soldiers. "It's a new cocktail," I said decisively, "the Alaska cocktail." "Do you like it?" he asked his soldiers. "It's awesome!" they all answered in unison, grinning widely, to the great satisfaction of their commander.

In Russian and in Polish, the word *voda* means water. The "-ka" suffix forms a diminutive, so "vodka" means "little water." The volume of the spirit produced during the distillation process is much smaller than the initial quantity of water used to make it, and that's probably where the beverage—which looks like water—got its name.

GIN

4 |

Juniper berry
one of the components of gin

"Gin Lane" (detail), engraving by William Hogarth, 1751

GIN IN A BOTTLE

Gin is having a moment. Though it fell off the radar for a while, and was even considered unfashionable, new and unusual gin brands are now proliferating all over the world. It's a gin-fest. The trend originated in Europe, and is particularly strong in Spain. Madrid is full of gin bars, with rich menus carrying many varieties of gin, and lots of different types of tonic to pair with them. Even the US has caught gin fever, and we're seeing a sharp uptick in the number of premium American gin labels.

It's not really clear why gin is experiencing a comeback, but it might have something to do with the dozens of boutique distilleries that have recently popped up in Europe. The original purpose of these distilleries was to produce whisky, but in an effort to increase their income during the long period of time that it takes for whisky to age, the distillery owners decided to distill gin, which is a simpler spirit that takes much less time to produce. The public has embraced this concept.

Is the gin revival just a passing trend, or is there something deeper going on here? Only time will tell. But let's first take a look at how it all began. In 1568 the Eighty Years' War broke out between the Netherlands and Spain. During the war, Dutch soldiers suffered from many illnesses because of poor sanitation. Diseases of the digestive system, the kidneys and the urinary tract were rampant. According to legend, Franciscus Sylvius—a Dutch physician and professor of medicine at the University of Leiden—decided to do something about it. So he took oil that he had extracted from juniper berries (*Juniperus*) and diluted it with alcohol. Leaves and seeds from the juniper plant had been used for medicinal purposes since many years before, dating back to the time the Black Death killed millions in Europe.

The juniper plant was used as a diuretic, and the alcohol as an anesthetic, and the doctor thought that combining the two would be good for treating soldiers' ailments. But the good doctor's experiment produced an unexpected result: The juniper berry oil made the distilled alcohol easier to swallow, and even tasty. Dr. Sylvius called the new elixir *jenever* (pronounced *ye-NAY-ver* in Dutch), and started to produce it in large quantities for soldiers. The "medicine" was quickly embraced by alcohol enthusiasts—even those who did not suffer from kidney problems—and became very popular in Dutch pubs.

The British fought alongside the Dutch in the Eighty Years' War, and quickly discovered the jenever through their comrades in arms. On the eve of a battle against the Spaniards, Dutch soldiers would turn to jenever to dull their fear. They would gulp it down to give themselves courage, and then went full force against their enemies. The British adopted the same approach. Jenever helped fighters forget about the horrors of war, and when the war was over they brought the drink back home with them to England. There, they changed the name of the beverage to "gin", and they made a few modifications to the production process. In particular, they added a few more ingredients to the distilled alcohol: Besides juniper berry oil, British gin was infused with spices such as cinnamon, ginger, angelica, caraway seed, cardamom, cloves, and coriander, in addition to peanuts, citrus fruits, and other flowers, plants, and roots.

During that same period, William of Orange, who was of Dutch descent, became the king of England and closed the borders of the country to French trade. This meant that the British had to find substitutes for the French wine and brandy they were used to. They turned to the new Dutch beverage. And because gin was cheap—unlike beer, which was heavily taxed during that time—it became a runaway success. At the beginning of the 18th century, 90 liters of gin were being produced in England per year, even though the country's population consisted of only 7 million people.

Because gin contained cheap ingredients and was priced affordably, most drinkers of the beverage were from the lower class. In fact, many people distilled low-quality gin in their own homes. This practice became so common that one home out of four in England was a makeshift gin distillery. The phenomenon attained such epic proportions that the period became well known as the "Gin Craze." The drink helped the oppressed to escape their bitter reality. Yet the gin also made their reality that much darker: Men, women and children stumbled drunk through the streets; babies suckled alcohol with their mothers' milk; and crime was rampant. Some of these scenes have been preserved in engravings made by the artist William Hogarth during that period. The etching *Gin Lane* portrays a street full of incapacitated drinkers. In the foreground we see a drunken mother, whose baby is falling out of her hands, over the railing of a stairway.

The authorities tried to combat the problem by imposing limitations and heavy taxes on liquor, but these only made distillers produce their liquor in secret. The British Parliament realized that their tactics were ineffective, and relaxed the regulations over time. This encouraged many distillery owners to produce higher-quality and more refined gin. As the quality of the beverage improved, dry gin became more common, and it started rising in social status and entered the homes of noblemen and statesmen. Very quickly, gin started to be exported across the ocean, to the many regions of the "empire on which the sun never sets." That was how India became a producer of gin, and how the beverage made it to Africa and North America. In the tropical regions of the Empire, and particularly in India, southeast Asia, and Africa, British soldiers who were being treated for the diseases that were common in those areas combined their medicine with gin-based drinks to improve the flavor. The British government was particularly concerned about malaria, which killed many soldiers, and therefore asked beverage producers to create a drink for soldiers that contained quinine, a medication used to treat the disease.

Jacob Schweppe accepted the challenge. Schweppe was the inventor of an efficient system for producing carbonated water, which ultimately developed into the Schweppes Factory. The quinine-containing beverage he came up with was called tonic water—carbonated water with quinine—and it was to be mixed with gin. The tonic water that was initially produced for medicinal purposes contained quite a large amount of quinine. Over time, tonic began to be consumed for non-medicinal purposes, and to be produced with smaller amounts of quinine. Nowadays, commercially-available tonic contains only a very small amount of quinine, which gives it its light and pleasantly bitter flavor.

The combination of gin and tonic has become one of the world's most popular mixed drinks. In recent years a large industry has emerged around the production of many different types of tonic and other mixers for "long drinks", which is the collective name for alcoholic beverages that are mixed with soft drinks and served in highball glasses. Gin is considered to be difficult to drink neat, so it is customary to dilute it with other beverages or to incorporate it into cocktails. Any self-respecting establishment that serves gin also carries tonic, because the two almost always go together.

During the Prohibition era in the US, pubs carried illicitly-produced gin that was not of particularly high quality. To mask the crude flavor, they would add a few drops of vermouth. The Italian Mafia maintained good ties with its homeland and smuggled in superior-quality Martini vermouth. When the Prohibition ended, the gin-vermouth combination turned into the most famous martini cocktail in the world. The classic, dry version of the martini contains a large amount of gin and a small amount of vermouth. Until the 1950s and 1960s gin continued to be a key player in the world of alcohol, but then, in the 1970s, vodka surpassed it as the most popular beverage. Gin's status continued to fade over a few decades, until very recently. Today the gin industry is rehabilitating quickly and acquiring a loyal customer base.

The GIN Shop.

"— now Oh dear, how shocking the thought is
They makes the gin from aquafortis :

They do it on purpose folks lives to shorten
And tickets it up at two-pence a quartern."

New Ballad

Designed Etched & Pub.d by Geo: Cruikshank — November 1st 1829.

A satirical sketch on the dangers of drinking alcohol, George Cruikshank

James Burrough

BEEFEATER GIN

The story of Beefeater Gin, one of the leading gin brands in the world, begins in 1862, when James Burrough, a pharmacist by trade, purchased a distillery in London's Chelsea neighborhood for 400 pounds. He started producing his own gin there in 1863. Burrough's father was a British tea merchant, and Burrough was intimately acquainted with different spices and leaves—so it is perhaps not surprising that he took naturally to gin. At first, Burrough continued to produce the beverages that the distillery had manufactured before he took over, to satisfy his preexisting customers. Still, from time to time, he experimented with new types of gin. After much trial and error, and many attempts to create new combinations of botanical ingredients, Burrough successfully produced the aromatic and full-flavored gin he was looking for. He called it "Beefeater", after the red-uniformed guards at the Tower of London, and a picture of a guard appears on the bottle's label. The beverage rose to popularity very quickly, and soon became the Burrough distillery's flagship product. The distillery was family-run until 1987, when it was sold to the Pernod Ricard corporation.

One of the people who has helped to preserve Burrough's legacy is the master distiller Desmond Payne, a world-renowned gin expert who has been working in the distillation business for 40 years. About 150 years after the original Beefeater had been distilled for the first time, Payne developed Beefeater 24, in a process that took 18 months, and introduced a wonderful premium beverage into the newly-trendy world of gin. Beefeater 24 contains 12 botanical ingredients, collected from various places all over the world. The ingredients are steeped together in a still for 24 hours—which is the origin of the name.

Singapore Sling

London-produced Beefeater gin is said to have inspired the classic Singapore Sling cocktail. According to legend, the cocktail was first mixed in the year 1915 by a bartender named Ngiam Tong Boon, who worked in a hotel called Raffles in Singapore. At first the cocktail was called the "gin sling" (a "sling" is a general term for a spirit mixed with water, sugar, and bitters). Over time, the beverage evolved to become much more complex and sweet (though still easy to prepare), and to incorporate many more ingredients—including, for example, pineapple juice, cherry liqueur, lime, Bénédictine, and orange liqueur. The beverage's composition has changed over the years, and there are countless versions of it all over the world. It was a huge hit in the 1980s. In the movie *Cocktail*, the bartender Brian Flanagan, played by Tom Cruise, recites a poem he wrote in which he mentions the Singapore Sling.

What you need
(for one highball glass)

40 ml gin
20 ml Heering cherry liqueur
5 ml orange liqueur
5 ml Bénédictine
10 ml grenadine
80 ml pineapple, lychee or passion
    fruit juice
30 ml lemon juice
A few drops of Angostura bitters
Cherry for garnish

What to do

Shake all the ingredients together in a shaker with ice and pour into a glass. Garnish with the cherry. Some people like to add seltzer.

Angostura bitters: An alcoholic mixture that is used to add a bitter and aromatic flavor to cocktails.

Hanky Panky

The Hanky Panky cocktail was invented by Ada "Coley" Coleman, who was the head bartender at the famous Savoy Hotel in London. Her patron was Rupert D'Oyly Carte, a member of a well-known London family that produced comic operas by Gilbert and Sullivan. D'Oyly Carte's family also erected several famous buildings in London, including the Savoy Hotel. The Savoy was the first luxury hotel in the UK with amenities such as electric lights, elevators, ensuite bathrooms, and hot and cold running water.

The hotel's entertainment staff included famous names such as George Gershwin and Frank Sinatra, and the hotel hosted many famous guests as well, including Charlie Chaplin, Judy Garland, Laurence Olivier, Marilyn Monroe, Humphrey Bogart, and Elizabeth Taylor. In 1903 Coleman got a job at the hotel bar, and eventually became the head bartender. She invented special cocktails for the celebrities who visited the hotel, including drinks for Mark Twain and for the Prince of Wales. One evening Charles Hawtrey, a famous actor at the time, arrived at the bar very tired and asked for a cocktail that would wake him up. When Coleman served him the cocktail she'd made for him, the actor took a sip and exclaimed, "By Jove! That is the real hanky-panky!" And that was how the cocktail got its name.

The Hanky Panky is a kind of sweet martini, but the invigorating ingredient that Coleman added was Fernet Branca, a very bitter Italian digestif, which turned the beverage into a unique cocktail in its own right.

**What you need
(for one cocktail glass)**

45 ml gin
45 ml red vermouth
A drizzle of Fernet Branca
An orange peel for garnish

What to do

Stir the ingredients in a shaker and pour into the glass. Lightly squeeze the orange peel above the cocktail and garnish with a twist of the peel.

Ad for Hendrick's Gin (detail), early 21st century

HENDRICK'S GIN

Hendrick's Gin was the brainchild of a whisky distiller at the Glenfiddich distillery, owned by William Grant & Sons. The distiller, who was a devoted gin lover (a fact that he probably kept secret), was having lunch on one of Scotland's few days of fine weather, holding a cucumber sandwich in one hand and a glass of gin in the other—and realized that he was very much enjoying the combination. He then had the brilliant idea of replicating that experience in a single drink. After much experimentation, and with the aid of two ancient stills that had been purchased several decades earlier by Charles Gordon, the owner of William Grant & Sons, he created a special gin with an aroma of cucumber.

Given that he was already famous as a whisky distiller, the gin's inventor preferred to remain anonymous. So the honor of choosing a name for the gin was bestowed upon Charles Gordon's mother, who was about to celebrate her 99th birthday. As was appropriate for a British noblewoman, the lady used the opportunity to pay tribute to Hendrick, the loyal gardener who had tirelessly taken care of her rose garden for 30 years.

In 1999 the master distiller Lesley Gracie began to produce Hendrick's Gin in two stills at a distillery in southwest Scotland. The gin contains several botanical ingredients, including juniper berries from Italy, caraway seed from the Netherlands, chamomile from Germany, coriander from Morocco, orris root from Morocco and Peru, cubeb berries from Indonesia, rose petals from Bulgaria, crushed green cucumbers that have been infused in cold water, and more. All these combine to create a fragrant and refreshing gin, which comes in an attractive and authentic-looking apothecary bottle.

"Reminds me of my safari in Africa.
Somebody forgot the corkscrew
and for several days we had to live
on nothing but food and water."

W. C. Fields, American comedian

Gin and Tonic

The traditional combination of gin and tonic, which is popular all over the world, originated in Britain. British soldiers started drinking gin after being introduced to its Dutch ancestor, the jenever, during the Eighty Years' War. The tonic came later: It was invented to help British soldiers serving in Asia, who needed to drink quinine as treatment for malaria. To help the bitter medicine go down, the quinine was mixed with soda water, and the combination was called "tonic" (which is just another word for medicine). The tonic was mixed with gin, together with lime to soften the bitter taste, and that's how one of the world's best-known mixed drinks was born.

The classic tonic that most of us are familiar with has a slightly sweet flavor. Nowadays, however, many bars carry a variety of high-quality dry tonics, to mix with gin according to your own personal preference. Spain is something of a world leader on the gin-and-tonic front, and Spanish bars offer dozens of gin brands alongside dozens of tonic brands, which bartenders are taught to pair according to the specific flavor profile of the gin. This means that customers can get exposed to many different nuances of gin and tonic, and the consumption experience becomes a lot more interesting. Some bars in Israel offer local tonic brands, some of which were concocted by the bar owners themselves, or by crazy people in their own homes—and each brand has its own unique aroma.

What you need
(for one highball glass)

60 ml gin
Tonic
Ice
A lemon slice

What to do

Put ice in the glass; pour in the gin. Add as much tonic as you like (between 20 and 120 ml) and the lemon slice.

The company that makes Hendrick's Gin suggests adding a slice of cucumber to the cocktail instead of a slice of lemon.

Gin Basil Smash

This refreshing summer cocktail was created in Hamburg, Germany, in a bar named Le Lion. The bartender, Jörg Meyer, was influenced by whisky "smash" cocktails that he had encountered at a bar in New York. In the summer of 2008 he invented this gin-based smash cocktail. Word about the new drink traveled fast through bars in Germany, and in no time the cocktail was crowned Best New Cocktail at the 2008 Tales of the Cocktail Spirited Awards.

The cocktail involves a relatively new technique called "muddling", in which you crush the ingredients—in this case, basil and lemon—together at the bottom of the glass.

What you need
(for one lowball glass)

60 ml gin
½ a lemon
3 large leaves of fresh basil
30 ml lemon juice
10 ml syrup (sugar water with
    a ratio of 1 part sugar to 1
    part water)
Ice
A basil leaf for garnish

What to do

Muddle the lemon and basil in a shaker.
Fill the shaker with ice and pour in the gin, lemon juice and syrup. Shake.
Strain twice, making sure to incorporate all ingredients by mashing them with a spoon. Pour the cocktail into a glass with ice, and garnish with the basil leaf.

TANQUERAY GIN

The year 1830 marked several breakthroughs for the world of alcohol. In that year, Aeneas Coffey invented the industrial method of continuous distillation in Scotland, pushing the alcohol industry a giant step forward. It was also the year in which Charles Tanqueray put the finishing touches on the fine new gin he had been developing. After years of testing many different botanical ingredients, he was ready to begin production. When he heard about the new continuous-distillation method, he decided to combine it with the traditional "Old Tom" distillation method to achieve the best possible result. Tanqueray's original secret recipe, written in his own handwriting, is still around today—and it is stored in a sealed black box inside a safe locked with three different combination locks, for which only three people know the combinations.

Tanqueray's gin was a huge success in Britain, and became renowned all over the world when British travelers to the Empire's colonies took it with them as provisions for the journey. Even the shape of its bottle was distinctive, resembling a 19th-century British fire hydrant. Tanqueray is considered to be one of the first registered trademarks in the world. Nowadays the gin is produced at a distillery in Scotland, and it is even produced in the original still, Old Tom, which has continued to operate despite sustaining damages in World War II. Tanqueray Gin has acquired many famous fans over the years, including Winston Churchill, John Kennedy, Ernest Hemingway, Frank Sinatra, and others, and it is featured in a number of songs, including songs by Bruce Springsteen, Keith Richards, Amy Winehouse, Madonna, and many rappers.

Charles Tanqueray

Martini Cocktail

"Martini" is a name for a family of classic cocktails based on gin. The original martini cocktail has remained consistently popular since its invention, and the drink even has a special cocktail glass named after it.

According to legend, the martini was invented around 1850. A California miner who had struck gold was heading back home to San Francisco, and he stopped at a town called Martinez along the way. Hoping to celebrate his success, the miner walked into a bar and ordered a glass of Champagne—but in a town in the middle of nowhere on the West Coast there was no Champagne. The bartender said he would make something even better and gave the miner a drink he called the "Martinez Special." The miner enjoyed it so much that he treated everyone at the bar to a round.

When the miner got to San Francisco he went into a local bar and asked for the drink he had enjoyed so much, but, of course, the bartender wasn't familiar with it. The miner explained how to make it, and the bartender tried it, fell in love, and began to make it for his friends and customers. Over time, the name of the drink was shortened to "martini."

The martini was quickly embraced by drinkers from all walks of life. Winston Churchill, one of the world's best-known martini drinkers, liked his martinis extra-extra dry. He used to fill his glass with gin, place a bottle of vermouth on the table, and look at it while he drank the gin. James Bond, Ian Fleming's fictional hero, helped put the martini on many menus, thanks to his habit of ordering a vodkatini—a martini based on vodka rather than gin. The author Dorothy Parker, comedian Harpo Marx's longtime drinking buddy, wrote a famous poem in honor of the cocktail:
  "I like to have a martini,
  Two at the very most.
  After three I'm under the table,
  after four I'm under my host."

What you need
(for one martini glass)

60 ml gin
10 ml dry white vermouth
Ice
A green olive on a toothpick
for garnish

What to do

Fill the glass with ice.
Pour the gin and the vermouth
into a shaker with ice and stir with
a spoon until the shaker becomes
cold. Remove the ice from the
glass and strain the cocktail into
the glass.
Garnish with the green olive
on a toothpick.

The ratio of vermouth to gin determines how dry the cocktail is. The lower the ratio, the drier the cocktail. In a so-called dry martini you only add a few drops of vermouth to the gin. If you replace the olive with a cocktail onion, the drink is called a Gibson. The TV series *Mad Men* frequently features both martinis and Gibsons.

Martini cocktail (see p. 100)

Fitzgerald

Dale DeGroff is one of the most famous New York bartenders of recent memory. He was a bartender at the Rainbow Room, that mythological New York institution that opened in the late '80s, and during his tenure there he created a menu of new and inventive cocktails, including the refreshing Fitzgerald.

DeGroff was a pioneer of the trend of returning to classic cocktails, and the Fitzgerald is a true classic. A simple summer cocktail, it's based on two summer staples—gin and tonic—with some sour and Angostura bitters added to the mix. DeGroff named the cocktail "Fitzgerald" in honor of F. Scott Fitzgerald, one of the greatest American authors of all time.

What you need
(for one lowball glass)

60 ml gin
30 ml lemon juice
20 ml sugar water (ratio of 1 part
    sugar to 1 part water)
A dash of Angostura bitters
Ice
Lemon peel twist

What to do

Combine all ingredients in a shaker with ice. Shake, then strain into the glass.
Squeeze the lemon peel slightly. The essential oils it releases will soften the bitter flavor of the gin. Garnish with the lemon twist.

"People who drink to drown their sorrow should be told that sorrow knows how to swim."

Ann Landers,
US journalist and editor

F. Scott Fitzgerald (1896–1940) was one of the greatest American authors of the 20ᵗʰ century, and he wrote about the "Roaring Twenties" in his novels and short stories. He is considered to be an icon of the "Lost Generation", people who were born at the end of the 19ᵗʰ century and came of age during World War I. Fitzgerald's most famous novel is *The Great Gatsby*, which has been adapted many times into film, most recently a film starring Leonardo DiCaprio as the title character.

Scott and his wife Zelda were a glamorous couple, celebrities of the '20s, and stars of the night club circuit, which was known for jazz music, Charleston dancing, and cocktails—which flowed as freely as they did in the underground speakeasies that were operating illegally during the Prohibition era. The couple's glamorous lifestyle ended tragically: Zelda was committed to a mental asylum, and Scott died at age 44, sick and an alcoholic.

F. Scott Fitzgerald

YOKHUS THE HOARSE

When Yokhus the Hoarse was born, his cry was so raspy that it overpowered the screams of his mother in labor and grated on the ears of everyone in the delivery room. That's when the midwife gave him his nickname: Hoarse. The nickname didn't prevent him from becoming an incredible pianist and rocking bars in Israel every Thursday night, belting out folk songs with his gravelly voice.

Yokhus the Hoarse was a big, strong man, with a thick beard and an even thicker neck, the product of many years of manual labor at the Port of Haifa. Over time his life story somehow became common knowledge: He had once been a sailor; he had once owned his own pub; later, he'd become a truck driver, transporting food all over Israel. He didn't look like the gentle type you'd expect to see playing piano and singing, but that wasn't the only surprising thing about him.

The first time I was introduced to him, Yokhus the Hoarse approached the bar and said: "Gas me and I shall qirsh you; change me with your mills." "What?!" I stared at him, baffled. "What did you say?" And he repeated the sentence. Later, I learned what it meant: Hayim Nahman Bialik, Israel's national poet, had spoken these words to a woman working at the first kiosk in Tel Aviv: "Pour me a soda (gaseous beverage = "gas me"), and I shall pay you with a qirsh (the main currency); then give me the change in mills (small change in local currency)." I fell in love. Who talks like that nowadays?

And he continued: "Mira, you battle mare, pour me a dram of the beverage you hold and I shall devour but a morsel, so as not to go hungry. I will recline at the bar, at your pleasure, and pray do serve me that morsel, a side of beef or two," meaning, two steaks. He didn't just like to eat, he liked to drink as well. He'd gulp down one gin and tonic after another, "just to moisten my throat." And once his throat was sufficiently moist, he'd start spinning his yarns.

And here is one of the stories he told me at the bar: "When I was serving in the merchant marine, I arrived one evening at a pier in Bermuda, docked my ship, and started attending to important business—such as consuming alcohol at the pub on the port. It was twilight, the place was quiet, and I sat at the piano they had there, playing for my pleasure. Little by little, people began to gather around the piano. After I had entertained them with songs from my repertoire, a young Englishman approached me and asked me if I wanted to continue playing at a party he was hosting at his home, on one of the hills. The man promised that the food and drink would be nothing short of a revelation, and he promised to get me back to my ship in time. It was difficult to refuse, and we drove to his house. There I found a very merry group of men and women, at varying stages of drunkenness. Beer, a piano, whisky, and high spirits; what could be better? The hours ticked by and the levels of alcohol rose. At some point I looked up at the clock and discovered that it was 2 a.m. I told my host that I had to get back to my ship. The Englishman said that in his condition he couldn't drive me there, but he gave me the keys to his motorcycle and asked me to leave it at the port. I got on the motorcycle and drove it about as fast as one drives a golf cart downhill, until I reached the main highway.

"While I was driving, I noticed a car coming directly at me in my lane, about to run me down. I pulled over to the shoulder, collected myself for a few moments, and got back on the road. Seconds later, yet another car was coming directly at me. Once again, I escaped to the shoulder in time. After the third car went by I realized that there must be some kind of misunderstanding, unless running down motorcycle riders was the national sport in Bermuda. I stopped for a moment, and through the fog of alcohol I managed to recall that Bermuda is a British island, and that British people have this strange habit of driving on the wrong side of the road. Very slowly, I made it to the port, where I put the keys to the motorcycle under the seat and added a note to my host, thanking him for the wonderful evening."

RUM

5

Flower of sugarcane
one of the components of rum

Slaves on a sugarcane plantation in the Caribbean, c. 1880

SAILORS, SLAVES AND PIRATES

Rum, the second-most-popular spirit in the world (the most popular spirit is vodka, in case you were wondering), is distilled from sugarcane. Most rum brands are manufactured in the Caribbean islands and near the estuary of the Demerara River in Guyana (previously British Guiana) in South America. The people living in these regions attribute powerful cultural and even religious significance to rum. In the local religion, Santeria, rum is commonly offered as a sacrifice to the gods.

Rum first started to be produced in the 15th century, but it got its name many years later. According to one legend, the name was given by British soldiers who arrived at Barbados and called the drink "rumbullion", which, in the slang at the time, meant "pandemonium." Over time the name got shorter and only the first syllable remained. Another story suggests that sailors traveling the world during the European Age of Exploration would drink the beverage in large goblets called "rummers", a word derived from the Dutch word *roemer*, which means "drinking glass."

The Caribbean islands are traditionally considered to be the birthplace of real rum: Slaves working on sugarcane plantations in Barbados discovered that they could produce alcohol by fermenting molasses, a by-product of sugarcane. Later they discovered that they could distill the fermented molasses to create a strong and highly aromatic alcoholic beverage.

The tradition of rum production in Cuba began in 1493, when Columbus and other explorers who followed him to the New World brought sugarcane to the island. The sweet plant thrived in Cuba's climate and fertile soil, and the sugar industry flourished. By 1620 there were already more than

50 distilleries producing rum from sugar. Soon enough, rum spread to South America and to European colonies in Central and North America, where it became highly popular. In the 18th century, rum consumption in the colonies was very high. The rise in demand for sugar throughout the world, and especially in Europe, led to more and more sugarcane plantations being established in the Caribbean islands, which created a need for more workers, and led to a sharp increase in trafficking of slaves from Africa. The molasses that the slaves produced was distilled into rum in the colonies, and the rum was used to pay for more slaves to be brought in from Africa. This so-called "triangular trade" of slaves, sugar, and rum was highly profitable for the colonies in the Americas. The influx of slaves from Africa to the Caribbean islands and to South America influenced the composition of the population in those areas, as well as the cultural practices.

Rum, more than any other beverage, is strongly associated with stories of pirates and the slave trade, mainly because of stories such as Robert Louis Stevenson's *Treasure Island*. And the tales are inspired by historical fact: Pirates used to steal ships carrying rum traders who were on their way to Europe or Africa, and would trade the ships for slaves whom they would sell to work on the sugar plantations in the Caribbean islands.

Rum's popularity wasn't limited to the colonies. For 300 years, beginning in the year 1655, rum was legally required to be supplied to sailors in Britain's Royal Navy as a morale booster. The daily ration, or "tot", was half a pint of undiluted rum, with an alcohol concentration of 47.75%. It was only on July 31, 1970 that the Royal Navy decided to eliminate the rum rations, claiming that times had changed, and that there was no justification for continuing the tradition, which might endanger sailors or cause them to commit unnecessary errors. On that day, called "Black Tot Day", many long-time sailors decided to retire early from the Royal Navy.

At the beginning of the 19th century, the quality of rum, which was originally very coarse, improved immensely after distillers began to use copper stills and to age the rum in barrels or in ceramic jugs. By the second half of the 19th century, rum had become known as a lighter, softer and more delicate beverage.

HAVANA CLUB

Havana Club, Cuba's national rum brand, is one of the most popular brands of rum in the world. It is produced in the city of Santa Cruz del Norte, and it is one of Cuba's most effective ambassadors. The Havana Club distillery was established in 1878 by Jose Arechabala. In 1959, after the Cuban Revolution, the Cuban government nationalized the distillery, and in 1993 the government entered into a 50:50 joint partnership with the Pernod Ricard corporation for the production and marketing of the beverage. Havana Club's logo features the Giraldilla, a bronze statue that looks out over Havana Harbor. The statue was poured in 1634, and, according to legend, it is the image of Isabel de Bobadilla, a beautiful Cuban woman whose husband set sail to find the Fountain of Youth in 1539, and never returned. The figure, called "Bella Havana" (beautiful Havana), became the unofficial mascot of the city of Havana, and an inseparable part of Havana Club's brand.

The Havana Club distillery in Cuba produces a large variety of rums from high-quality sugarcane, in accordance with Cuban tradition. Each one of the brand's labels is aged for a different period of time, through a natural aging process in wood barrels. The selection of barrels is critical, because the type of wood and the extent to which it is toasted affect the aroma, the flavor, and the texture of the final product. Havana Club Añejo 7, which is aged for seven years, is the company's flagship product and the best representative of the complex art of distilling rum.

During World War II, Roosevelt's efforts to establish more open trade relations with the Caribbean Islands, with Latin America in general and with Cuba in particular, made rum available throughout the US, and rum-based cocktails became highly popular. Several famous rum enthusiasts included the author Ernest Hemingway and John F. Kennedy, the 35th president of the United States. Rum was no longer the domain of sailors alone; it had been embraced by tastemakers, poets, tourists, and partygoers.

The Cuba Libre, or the rum and coke, is the most popular rum-based cocktail in the world. According to legend, in 1961, when tensions were high between the US and Cuba, ultimately leading to a breakdown of diplomatic relations between the two countries, Fidel Castro stood on a large balcony and spoke to the Cuban people. Castro condemned products produced by American capitalism, and when he finished his speech he took a glass, poured rum in it, added Coca Cola, the epitome of capitalism—perhaps implying that the bottle was the last one that would ever enter Cuba—and cried, "Cuba Libre!" ("Cuba is free!"). The crowd cheered and shouted the words back to him, and that's how the Cuba Libre was born.

The Giraldilla at Havana Harbor, Cuba

"[An] intelligent man is
sometimes forced to be
drunk to spend his time
with fools."

Ernest Hemingway,
For Whom the Bell Tolls

Ernest Hemingway

The author Ernest Hemingway (1899–1961) was one of rum's most prolific publicists: He not only mentioned rum in his books but also made it famous through his personal lifestyle. Hemingway moved from the US to Paris in the 1920s, where he lived alongside many other well-known ex-pat writers, poets, and artists, including James Joyce, Gertrude Stein, Ezra Pound, Pablo Picasso, and many others. The ex-pats would frequent a bar called Harry's New York Bar and drink large amounts of alcohol in general and Bloody Marys in particular. They called themselves the "Lost Generation", a name that Gertrude Stein came up with.

When his books started to be successful, Hemingway began to spend most of his time fishing, drinking absinthe (an anise-based drink), and occasionally writing. After recovering from the Spanish Civil War, Hemingway spent most of World War II on his boat, named *Pilar*, which was equipped with a radio, a lot of rum, and a few weapons. The boat was part of the "Hooligan Navy", a makeshift navy organized by the US government, made up of civilians who owned private boats, which would go after German submarines that approached the shores of the US and Cuba.

In 1944 Hemingway gladly returned to liberated Paris to his regular bar. There, he celebrated with his friends with more than a week of nonstop drinking. In the 1950s, after Hemingway won the Nobel Prize for Literature, his excessive drinking started to take its toll on his writing and his behavior. He became an alcoholic and suffered from severe depression, from which he never recovered. Ultimately, he shot himself, as his father had done before him, just a few weeks before his 62nd birthday.

Daiquiri

Many local legends have been told about the daiquiri. Just about every other bar in the Caribbean claims to have invented the cocktail. The most commonly accepted origin story is that the classic form of the cocktail was first prepared in an iron mine in Cuba towards the end of the 19th century. The person who concocted it was a mining engineer named Jennings Stockton Cox, who chilled rum with ice (or water), lemons, and sugar. In 1909 Admiral Lucius Johnson, a US naval medical officer, tried it out and was so excited about the new cocktail that he began spreading the word to everyone in the Navy. From there, the daiquiri spread to Washington and to night clubs in New York.

The cocktail's name comes from the region of Daiquiri, where the drink was supposedly first prepared, and the word is from the language of the Taíno, an indigenous people of the Bahamas and the Antilles. The daiquiri became particularly popular during the 1940s, as rum sales increased during World War II because of the shortage of other beverages such as whisky or vodka.

What you need
(for one cocktail glass)

60 ml light rum
30 ml lime juice or
    sweetened lemon juice
Ice

What to do

Shake the ingredients together in a shaker and strain into a glass.

Some people prefer their daiquiris frozen. To make a frozen daiquiri, fill the cocktail glass with crushed ice and then strain the cocktail onto the ice. And for advanced mixologists: Blend the rum and lime or lemon juice in a blender with 10 ice cubes, together with the fruit of one's choice (strawberry, pineapple, lemon, apple, or whatever else), and pour into a glass.

Mojito

In the 16th century, to mask the crude flavor of pirate rum, sailors would add lime and mint, a step that apparently prevented many diseases. The beverage was called El Draque, after Sir Francis Drake, a famous pirate and English admiral. Several hundred years later, a bartender in Cuba mixed a similar drink and called it a mojito, and the drink's popularity began to rise.

As a rum lover, Ernest Hemingway was a fan of the mojito as well. When he lived in Havana he would drink mojitos in two bars that he frequented: Floridita and Bodegita del Medio. James Bond also famously ordered a mojito in the movie *Die Another Day*. The mojito is one of Cuba's flagship cocktails, and is a direct competitor to the Brazilian caipirinha.

What you need
(for one highball glass)

60 ml light rum
20 ml lime or lemon juice
10 mint leaves
2 teaspoons of sugar
 (preferably brown)
Soda water
A slice of lemon for garnish

What to do

Muddle the mint and sugar in a glass. Add the rum and lime or lemon juice and stir well.
Fill the glass up to 2/3 of its height with crushed ice or ice cubes, and top off with soda up to the rim of the glass. Garnish with the lemon slice.

THE GENEROUS GUY

"The Generous Guy" first visited our bar at a very early hour one evening. He came in, sat across from me at the bar, and didn't say a word. I turned to him, giving him the smile that I save for new people, and asked him what he wanted to drink. The guy puzzled over my question and finally said: "A very strong espresso." A strong espresso is often a promising sign of a long evening of drinking ahead, and I gave him a small cup of powerful coffee, per his request. I looked him over. He was in his 30s—late 30s—not bad looking, even though there was a certain deadness to his eyes. Maybe he was going through a rough time and had come to the bar to try to lift his spirits. His eyes followed me around, suggesting that he wanted to talk. *OK*, I thought, *No problem*. I like to talk and I like to listen, and I've turned this personality flaw into a profession.

Soon enough I had heard the guy's story, which was actually pretty interesting, though it was sometimes difficult to hear what he was saying over the bluster of his enormous ego. Throughout our conversation I would sneak looks at the cup of espresso. I've never seen anyone drink such a small amount over such a long time. The guy was not totally oblivious and explained that he actually really liked drinking and going out to bars, in Israel and abroad, but just now he was taking medication that prevented him from drinking alcohol.

After a disproportionately long time for a very short espresso, and an equally long conversation, the guy asked for the check. He paid for his espresso, and then reached into his wallet and pulled out a single shiny shekel (worth about 25 cents), and dropped it ceremoniously into the tip jar with a loud, sad clink. He left the bar with a self-satisfied smile, and I sighed and drowned my sorrows in a drink.

Later that week it happened again. The guy was still taking his mysterious medication; he ordered a strong espresso, talked about himself nonstop, and then repeated the ritual of dropping a shekel into the jar. The wait staff at the pub gave him a nickname: "The Generous Guy." Over the next few days I noticed that The Generous Guy would only toss his shekel into the jar after catching my eye to make sure I was watching. Without me there to witness the ceremony, he could not complete it. So of course, when the moment of truth arrived, I suddenly had a ton of things to do. I deserve to have fun, too. But the guy just waited; he refused to leave without having his moment. My *schadenfreude* went unfulfilled, and I had no choice but to participate in his annoying game.

How do you get rid of a guy like this? I asked myself. *Where is your famous sense of resourcefulness?* One evening the opportunity fell into my hands. The Generous Guy drank two espressos and asked for the check. "Fourteen shekels," I said, drily. Would he toss in two shekels for the two espressos? The Generous Guy pulled 15 shekels out of his wallet and handed it to me. I put the money in the register and kept the one shekel quietly in my hand. I didn't have the fortitude to watch the ceremony of the placement of the shekel in the jar. The guy continued to sit there. "Do you want anything else?" I asked. "Uh, no, I'm waiting for change." Bless his heart.

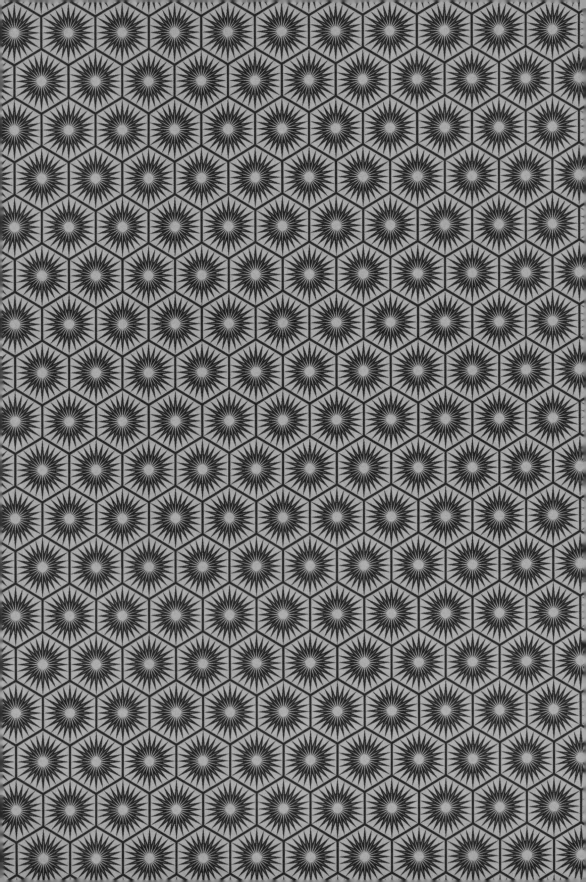

TEQUILA

6

Blue agave
one of the components of tequila

THE BLOOD OF THE GODDESS MAYAHUEL

The origin of the word "tequila" can be traced to the beginning of the 16th century. Some say that the beverage is named after a town called Tequila in Mexico, on the outskirts of the large city of Guadalajara, the tequila capital of the world. Others claim that the source of the name is the volcano Tetilla. Tequila is Mexico's national beverage and one of the country's largest and most important exports.

The Mexican government holds the rights to the name "tequila", and it has legislated strict laws that determine which beverages are eligible to be called by that name. According to the government's regulations, to be called a "tequila" a beverage must contain at least 51% fermented juice of the blue agave plant. The remaining 49% is made up of sugars that are added during the fermentation process, usually from sugarcane or molasses. Premium tequila brands are made of 100% agave, and these must be bottled inside Mexico in a process that is subjected to rigorous government oversight. Tequila can only legally be produced in five Mexican states: In the state of Jalisco, and in specific villages in four other states. Tequila-like beverages made outside those regions are called "mezcal." Every bottle of tequila must have a NOM identifier printed on it, a number that indicates the identity of the factory that produced the bottle. The alcohol concentration in tequila must be between 35% and 49% (most tequilas contain 38%–40% alcohol). Once all these conditions have been met, you can relax, take a sip, and say "tequila bueno" ("good tequila").

In Mexico, the agave plant has been in use for about 9,000 years, beginning with ancient civilizations that wove fabric out of its fibers. According to Mexican legend, the agave plant is a reincarnation of the goddess Mayahuel, and the honey-like sap contained in the plant is her blood. Another myth describes a bolt of lightning that hit an agave plant and cooked it with its heat. The sap of the cooked plant began to bubble, and its scent and flavor were so delicious that the people who saw it thought it must be a gift from the gods.

Before discovering agave nectar, the Mexican people had made beverages from plants such as corn and wild plums and from honey and tree bark. But the agave plant was considered to possess special qualities, and the first drink produced from it—the *pulque*—took on powerful mystical significance, symbolizing rebirth in nature, among other things. After the harvest, pulque was used in religious ceremonies to ensure a bountiful crop in the coming year. It was also used to bless new fields and buildings. As it was believed to have healing powers, it was used for medicinal purposes. Pulque was considered to be sacred, and only noble families and priests were permitted to drink it. Everyone else could only drink pulque on the Day of the Dead, a religious celebration that takes place at the end of each year.

The first Spanish conquistadors who arrived in Mexico discovered the pulque, which was sour and low in alcohol content, resembling beer. They distilled it and produced a beverage that they called mezcal wine. Supposedly, the drink was first produced near the town of Tequila (the name meant "work" in the local dialect).

The agave plant grows in 5 of the 32 states that make up the Federal Republic of Mexico. The most important one is the state of Jalisco, where the town of Tequila is located. The agave plant belongs to the amaryllis family, though a common misconception is that it belongs to the cactus family. The blue agave, which has blue-green leaves, is the only species of agave that is used to make tequila. The agave, similarly to the banana, grows as a "mother plant" that reproduces by spreading roots and offshoots. In cultivated agave, an offshoot that has grown for five years is cut off from the mother plant and replanted. In the sixth year the tips of the long leaves are trimmed, and the plant's tall flowering stalk is cut down, so that it does not draw sugar away from the heart of the plant. The heart, which is also called a *piňa* because of its resemblance to a large pineapple, typically weighs between 35 and 80 kilos.

In 1758 the king of Spain gave some land to Don Jose Antonio de Cuervo near the town of Tequila. Jose Cuervo raised agave plants and established a distillery on his land, where he became the first person to produce alcohol from cultivated agave. Initially, the Spanish forbade production of the drink, because they wanted Mexico to purchase its alcohol from Spain. But in 1795 the king granted the first license to produce alcohol locally. Many years after Don Jose started distilling his mezcal wine, additional distilleries started popping up, including the Sauza distillery, which began to export its products to the US in 1873. This really led tequila to take off, and the establishment of railroads in the area also contributed greatly to the development and exportation of the drink. And of course, thanks to Prohibition in the US, tequila was frequently smuggled across the border, to be sold in underground speakeasies.

After World War II tequila began to be introduced into other parts of the world. Sales expanded in the 1950s, when the margarita started to become popular. New customs started to appear, such as drinking tequila with lemon and salt: You sprinkle salt on the back of your hand between the thumb and index finger, lick it, drink the tequila in one shot, and then suck on or eat a lemon wedge. It's a winning flavor combination. The salt is supposed to soften the burn of the tequila by making the mouth produce saliva, and the lemon improves the flavor. The drink was perfect for young people who were looking to add a little kick to their drinking experience.

Portrait of Don Jose Antonio Cuervo. Painting by Francisco Goya, 1819

You won't find a worm in a bottle of tequila—rather, you'll find it in mezcal, which has a smokier flavor. The little worm, called a *gusano* in Spanish, is actually the larva of a moth. After all the mezcal has been drunk from the bottle, the person who was brave enough to down the last shot has to eat or suck on the worm. The worm doesn't have any special flavor; it's just saturated with alcohol. But according to myth it can alter the consciousness of the person who eats it and cause him or her to hallucinate.

Supposedly, the myth that the worm can make you trip is rooted in ancient legend that worms suck out the spirit of the holy agave plant and transmit it to the drinker. Actually, though, it's just a marketing gimmick invented by a mezcal merchant who decided to incorporate some mythology into his liquor. He put a worm into every bottle and added a small packet of salt, spices, chili powder, and ground worms. His drink, Gusano de Oro ("Worm of Gold"), was highly successful, and the legend was born.

For hundreds of years the moth larva was an important component of the local cuisine; it has a delicious flavor and a lot of nutritional value. The larva is commonly served fried with tomatoes and chili peppers. Mezcal is usually only drunk from a shot glass.

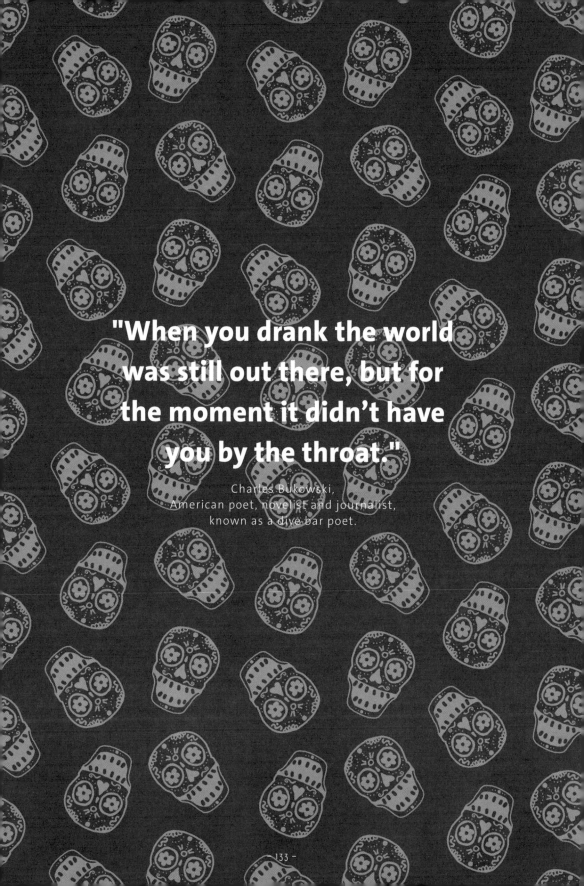

"When you drank the world
was still out there, but for
the moment it didn't have
you by the throat."

Charles Bukowski,
American poet, novelist and journalist,
known as a dive bar poet.

Margarita

The margarita is a classic all over the world. Many legends are told about this cocktail, some as exciting as the cocktail itself. Its most famous origin story starts with the actress Marjorie King, who, during the Prohibition Era of the 1920s and the early 1930s, would cross the border from California into Mexico to grab some forbidden drinks. One day the star was sitting in a restaurant in Tijuana, Mexico and announced to one and all that she was allergic to every alcoholic beverage except tequila—so the bartender made her a cocktail she could drink and named it "margarita" in her honor. According to another story, the inventor of the margarita was a woman named Margaret Sames, who would host celebrities at her private cliffside hacienda in Acapulco. To try to save a party that was going south, she mixed some tequila with Cointreau and lime juice. She dipped the rim of a glass in salt, and the margarita was born. And another interesting story: One Fourth of July in 1942, a talented bartender in Ciudad Juarez, named Pancho Morales, was asked by one of his regular customers to make a magnolia cocktail. Morales had never made the cocktail but remembered that it had Cointreau in it, so he mixed Cointreau with tequila and thus created the margarita. Some historians claim that Morales called the drink a "margarita", which means "daisy" in Spanish, because he got the names of the flowers confused.

What you need
(for one margarita glass)

60 ml tequila
30 ml Cointreau (orange liqueur)
30 ml lime juice
Ice
Lemon peel twist or a lemon slice
    for garnish

What to do

Fill the glass with ice. Shake all ingredients together in a shaker with ice. Remove the ice from the glass and strain the beverage into the glass. Garnish with the lemon slice or peel.

It is customary to dip the rim of the glass in lemon juice and then in salt.

Frozen Margarita

Unsurprisingly, in hot climates, blended frozen margaritas tend to be more popular than the classic version. The frozen margarita is usually served as a kind of "slushy" drink made with fresh fruit or fruit juice, tequila, and orange liqueur.

What you need
(for one large glass)

60 ml tequila
30 ml Cointreau (orange liqueur)
30 ml squeezed lime juice or
    lemon juice
Your favorite fruit, for example,
    a diced mango, 5-6 lychee fruits
    (either fresh or canned),
    5-6 strawberries, etc.
Ice

What to do

Combine all ingredients in a blender, blend and pour into the glass. Garnish with fresh fruit.

It is customary to dip the rim of the glass in lemon juice and then in salt.

Tequila Sunrise

This classic cocktail is somewhat outdated, and many trendy bars won't make it for you, but it still has quite a few fans throughout the world. The name "tequila sunrise" comes from the color of the drink, which looks like a sunrise. The heavy grenadine sinks to the bottom and colors the bottom of the glass red, and the orange juice poured on top gives it a yellow color.

What you need
(for one highball glass)

60 ml tequila
90 ml orange juice
10 ml grenadine
Ice
An orange slice for garnish

What to do

Pour the tequila and orange juice into a glass with ice; then add the grenadine. Garnish with the orange slice.

THE DEVIL'S BREW

According to a story in the *Midrash*, when the Flood ended and Noah planted his first vineyard, the devil asked to participate. To Noah's amazement, the devil proceeded to slaughter a sheep, a lion, a pig, and a monkey and watered the young vines with their blood. The devil explained to Noah that before a man has drunk wine he behaves like a sheep, calm and quiet. After drinking a little bit of wine he believes he is powerful like the lion. If he continues to drink, he will roll in the trash like a pig, and if he drinks even more he will completely lose control and go wild like a monkey.

Many other folklore traditions connect the devil to alcohol, which, in some legends, is referred to as "devil's water." In these tales, the devil uses alcohol to tempt people and lead them to sin—maybe because alcohol lowers inhibitions, and maybe as a hint of the dangers that people expose themselves to when they drink too much and lose control of their faculties.

The Serbs have an interesting variation on this idea. One Serbian legend tells that when God banished the first man from heaven, He burdened the man with immense worry, but the man could not take it and buried the worry in the ground. But the ground could not contain the worry either, and gave it to the mountain. The worry made the mountain begin to dry up, and it gave the worry to the rock, but the rock began to melt. So the worry went back to man. Men would have lost their minds with worry, were it not for the devil, who invented wine and drink. At first the devil built a structure on stilts at a crossroads, with a door on each side. In this place the devil turned the water into wine, stood at the entrance and began pouring wine for all the passersby, so they would not go mad with worry.

Source: *Serbian Mythology* by Dina Katan Ben-Zion, Mapa publishing, Israel, 2005

"Young Sick Bacchus" (detail), painting by Caravaggio, c. 1592

WHAT WILL THE LADY BE HAVING?

Reidel, our bar in the picturesque Israeli town of Zichron Yaakov, served quite a large variety of cocktails: the Brazilian caipirinha, for example, which was a huge hit in the late '90s, or arak with grapefruit juice and mint, which we served to try to make our customers love arak just as much as we did. So admittedly, with all those cocktails, it wasn't easy to choose just one. But we had no idea how truly difficult it could be.

One evening, the bar was bustling, and three sleepy young men were slumped over the bar. Suddenly, all three of them sat bolt upright and their eyes shot straight to the door. *Hottie alert*, I thought. I glanced at the door and, indeed, there was a woman standing there. Specifically, it was The Lady, as she was known to everyone in Zichron, an exceptionally good-looking and well-groomed woman.

The Lady looked around, trying to decide whether and where to sit down. I gave her a big, inviting smile, which helped her to decide, and she walked hesitantly over and sat down next to the guys. The men started chatting among themselves with feigned nonchalance, trying to hide their excitement. She stared at the menu for a long time, deliberating. The guys sitting next to her finished their araks with grapefruit juice, and she continued deliberating. She just couldn't decide on a drink.

"Maybe a caipirinha?" I asked.
"No, no thanks."
"Beer? Wine? Red? White?" I insisted.
"I'm treating this woman to a drink. Whatever she wants—it's on me," said one of the guys. The Lady gave me a meaningful look and then tossed back: "Actually... I... don't want anything today... I already brushed my teeth."

WHISKY

7

Barley
one of the components of whisky

SCOTCH: MALT OR BLENDED?

Scotch whisky (scotch) is one of the UK's five most profitable exports. Scotch producers claim that every second, 30 bottles of scotch are sold somewhere in the world. One out of six people in Scotland works in the whisky industry, and more than 100 distilleries are currently operating on the island. So it's perhaps appropriate that the Scots were the ones to come up with the term "angel's share" to refer to the amount of whisky, about 2%, that evaporates out of every barrel during the aging process. According to some estimates, about a million liters of whisky evaporate over Scotland every year, making the Scotland sky highly alcoholic. It seems like the perfect place for angels to gather to claim their share.

There are two main types of whisky. The first is malt whisky, which is made only out of malted barley and does not contain any other grains (such as wheat, corn, or rye). This is the traditional type of scotch whisky, and it is distilled the old-fashioned way, in copper stills. Adding the prefix "single"—as in "single malt"—means that the malt in the beverage comes from just one distillery. The flavor of this type of whisky is determined by where it comes from, much in the way that wines made from grapes of different regions have different flavors and personalities. Most single-malt whisky brands are produced in Scotland, but whisky is also made in Ireland (where it is spelled "whiskey"), in Japan, and elsewhere.

The other type of whisky is blended whisky, which combines different types of grains and malts. Blended whisky is distilled using a modern technique, invented in the 19th century, called continuous industrial distillation. Whisky produced in this way has a softer and more refined flavor compared with whisky that is produced in with traditional batch distillation. A blended whisky typically contains about 15 to 50 different types of whisky, which are combined together according to the distiller's own secret recipe. The purpose of mixing them is to extract as much as possible from each whisky, and to create a consistent beverage that is better than the sum of its parts.

Malt whisky's many fans tend to claim that their beverage of choice is superior to blended whisky. Indeed, malt, and especially single malt, is more prestigious, and is therefore more expensive. Be that as it may, malt lovers owe a debt of gratitude to blended whisky, because without it the fine malts they drink could not exist. Scottish whisky producers say that malt whisky gets all the glory, but blended whisky pays the bills, because the truth is that 95% of the whisky sold in the world is of the blended variety.

Whisky got its name from Gaelic, the language spoken by the ancient civilizations living in the British Isles. The source of the name is from the Gaelic words *uisge beatha* (in Scotland) or *uisce beatha* (in Ireland), which mean "water of life." Over time the name of the drink was abbreviated to *uisce* and to *ooshk*, and it mutated even further into the modern word "whisky."

William Grant and wife, late 19th century

GLENFIDDICH

The old-school malt whisky industry was almost nonexistent outside of Scotland until the 1960s. The Scots were convinced that foreigners' palates would never be able to get used to the flavorful and aromatic beverage, so they decided to export only malt's younger sibling, blended whisky.

The William Grant & Sons company decided to switch things up. In 1963, in a move that their colleagues at other distilleries thought was completely insane, professional suicide in fact, the company started exporting their flagship whisky Glenfiddich and revolutionized the world of alcohol. Malt whisky began to occupy its proper place in the world as a highly prestigious alcoholic beverage.

William Grant & Sons has always been a family operation. William Grant was a goat herder at age 7, and later he also became a shoemaker. When he grew up he studied accounting, but his true dream was to establish a whisky distillery that would make the best whisky in the world. At the young age of 27 he came close to his dream, when he started working at the Mortlach distillery. He worked there for 20 years and learned the secrets of whisky production. The money he managed to save from his meager salary eventually enabled him to fulfill his dream.

In 1886 Grant purchased a small patch of land in Dufftown, located by the River Fiddich ("the river of the deer") in the Speyside region in the heart of the Scottish Highlands. With his own two hands—and with the help of his wife and nine children—Grant built the whisky distillery he'd always dreamed of. On Christmas Eve in 1887 he finished distilling his first batch of whisky, which he named Grant's Glenfiddich, after the neighboring river.

The whisky he produced was highly successful, and in 1892 Grant opened another distillery nearby called Balvenie.

Grant's distillery was known for prizing creativity and innovation. In 1957 the designer Hans Schleger designed the distillery's unique triangular bottles, which were considered highly novel at the time. In 1963 the Glenfiddich distillery became the first to open its gates to visitors and tourists. But this was all nothing compared with the distillers' dramatic decision that the world was ready for single-malt Scotch whisky. They began to export Glenfiddich, paving the way for an entire industry.

The flavor of a malt whisky is affected by the wood of the barrel in which it is aged. For years, Scotch whisky was aged in barrels that previously contained sherry. When there weren't enough such barrels to go around, they started to use barrels that had previously contained American bourbon whiskey. The combination of the two types of barrels led to a discovery: the whisky's personality changed a little; it became more interesting and took on new flavors and aromas. In recent years, the Glenfiddich distillery has begun to "finish" its whisky in barrels that previously contained ale, a move that has proven to be highly popular all over the world.

The Glenfiddich distillery has also made history in the domain of aging spirits. One cask of whisky began the aging process in 1937 and was bottled only in 2001—setting a new world record. Only 61 bottles of that record-breaking 64-year batch were released into the world.

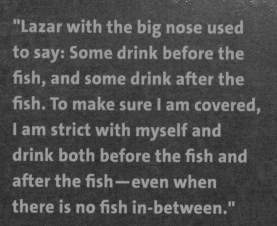

"Lazar with the big nose used
to say: Some drink before the
fish, and some drink after the
fish. To make sure I am covered,
I am strict with myself and
drink both before the fish and
after the fish—even when
there is no fish in-between."

Hassidic joke,
from the book *Druyanov's Book of Jokes and Wit*,
Dvir, Israel, 1964.

There are no hard and fast rules as to what types of whisky can be used in a whisky cocktail. Whisky zealots usually frown on mixing prestigious malt whisky in a cocktail. They believe that malt whisky should exclusively be served neat, to ensure it is given the respect it deserves. This means that whisky cocktails usually contain blended whisky. I think that the best way to enjoy classic whisky cocktails, which do not contain very many ingredients, is to use the whisky you like and are used to enjoying, whether it's blended whisky or a superior malt that will add complexity and personality to your drink. Glenfiddich, the beloved malt whisky that broke the glass ceiling and was the first to be exported to the world, is very soft and pleasant and can upgrade many different types of cocktails.

Whisky Sour

The whisky sour is, without a doubt, the most popular sour (sweet-and-sour) cocktail in the world. It's a classic, quick and easy to make. Two ingredients can take this cocktail to the next level: good whisky and fresh-squeezed lemon juice. Different types of whisky produce different flavors and experiences. In recent years it's become common to add an egg white to the mix and to shake it up for extra texture and thickness, without altering the flavor.

What you need
(for one lowball glass)

45 ml whisky
30 ml lemon juice, freshly squeezed
10 ml syrup (sugar water with a ratio
    of 1 part sugar to 1 part water)
Ice
Egg white (optional)
A cherry or lemon slice for garnish

What to do

Shake the ingredients together in a strainer with ice and pour into the glass.
Garnish with the cherry or lemon slice.

Blood and Sand

This cocktail is named after a popular silent film from the year 1922, starring Rudolph Valentino as a bullfighter who sets sail for a complicated adventure with a wealthy widow. Like the love affair in the movie, the Blood and Sand cocktail is made up of an unlikely combination of summer and winter ingredients: scotch, Heering cherry liqueur, orange juice, and sweet vermouth. The movie is based on a Spanish novel called *Sangre y Arena* (literally "blood and sand"), and yes, there's also a cocktail that bears the Spanish name, based on mezcal rather than whisky.

What you need
(for one cocktail glass)

30 ml whisky
20 ml red vermouth
20 ml Heering cherry liqueur
30 ml fresh-squeezed orange juice
Ice
Cherry for garnish

What to do

Fill the glass with ice. Shake all the ingredients together in a shaker with ice. Remove the ice from the glass and strain the cocktail into the glass. Garnish with the cherry.

ON WHISKY, TAXES, AND NATIONAL PRIDE

In Scotland, whisky is not just a drink; it's an integral part of the country's identity, tradition, customs and history. As such, for many Scots, whisky is a source of national pride and a symbol of independence, and the process of distilling it is considered an art unto itself. Whisky also has an integral role in Scotland's history and in its complicated relationship with Britain and, no less importantly, in its complicated relationship with taxes.

The first time whisky production was taxed in Scotland was in 1644, long before the country united with England. In that year, the Scottish Parliament, which was based in Edinburgh, imposed a tax on whisky and determined that whisky production and sales could no longer be unregulated as they had been until then. In those days, 90% of the population lived in rural areas and distilled whisky primarily for personal use, and, to a lesser extent, for sales. The independent distillers felt the tax to be an unfair burden, and they saw it as an attack on their freedom and pride. The authorities never really succeeded in enforcing the tax, and all the friction surrounding the issue just made the beverage more popular.

Until 1707, Scotland was still an independent kingdom, but then things changed. The same politicians in Edinburgh who had voted to tax whisky now voted to unite with England—a move that most of the population, and certainly those living in the countryside, were opposed to. Now that they were under the control of the Parliament in London, which imposed more and more laws and taxes, the Scots' opposition intensified. For them, the issue at stake was much more than just taxation; they perceived the Parliament's actions as violations of their honor and their independence. Opposing the already-unpopular whisky tax became a patriotic act and a symbol of resistance to foreign rule. More and more private distilleries began to be established and to operate illegally, creating an entire industry of whisky smuggling and tax evasion. The population cooperated with the smugglers, and the distilleries even cooperated with one another. And in this cat-and-mouse game, the British government was at a disadvantage. In 1823 the authorities gave up and changed the law. The new tax law was friendlier and more accommodating, and its effects manifested very quickly. The distilleries that, until then, had been operating covertly began to produce whisky out in the open and in accordance with the law. And because the distillers did not have to spend all their time evading taxes, the quality of the whisky improved immensely.

One of the least popular people in Scotland during the period when the despised tax laws were in effect was Aeneas Coffey, a customs officer from Dublin. In 1823, when the laws were repealed, Coffey quit his job and launched a new career: He became a distiller. Coffey saw how inefficient and slow the traditional batch distillation process was, so he invented and produced a machine that would distill whisky continuously, quickly, and at low cost. The system required less energy and maintenance than the traditional methods and could operate forever. One continuous-distillation setup could produce 9000 liters of spirit per day. This distillation method revolutionized the alcohol industry in general and the whisky industry in particular. And, of course, it changed the flavor of the whisky: Continuously-distilled whisky was softer and easier to drink compared with its older sibling. That's how blended whisky was born, and many people preferred its light flavor to that of whisky distilled traditionally. Nowadays, blended whisky makes up about 90% of the whisky produced in Scotland.

Is the color of whisky an indicator of its quality?
You might be disappointed to hear this, but the law
permits whisky manufacturers to add caramel coloring
to their whisky. That means that the color of whisky does
not necessarily reflect its quality.

Chivas distillery, mid-19th century

CHIVAS REGAL

Did you know that a bottle of Chivas Regal is sold every second, somewhere in the world? Chivas Regal is one of the best-known brands of whisky, and one of the first brands of blended whisky to be produced. Chivas is considered to be a strong contender in the premium whisky market, and in Europe it is the top-selling premium whisky. More than 30 million bottles of Chivas are sold per year in more than 150 countries all over the world.

The name "Chivas" comes from the Scottish Gaelic word *seamhas*, which means "lucky." Some people claim that "seamhas" actually means "narrow place beside a river." At one time, almost all the people living in the villages along the banks of the river Ythan in Aberdeenshire had the same last name: Chivas.

The story of Chivas Regal began with two brothers, James and John Chivas, who, together with their parents and their ten siblings, left the village for the big city. The family settled in Aberdeen in 1836. John worked in a clothing factory, and James sold food and drinks at a grocery. When the store owner died in 1841, James Chivas purchased the business together with another grocer named Charles Stewart.

The continuous-distillation method had recently been invented, and around that time many business owners were beginning to blend and sell their own whisky. Chivas and Stewart jumped on the bandwagon and blended a new type of whisky, bottled it, and sold it at the shop. They called the whisky Royal Glen Dee, named after the River Dee, on whose banks Queen Victoria of England had a vacation home. The blend became very popular in Aberdeen and was distributed from there to the rest of the British Isles.

In 1842, Queen Victoria visited Scotland for the first time. The palace ordered many items—including wine and alcohol, of course—from Chivas and Stewart's shop, which had expanded and grown since its modest early days. The royal family enjoyed their purchases so much that a year later they appointed James Chivas as the palace's head grocery supplier. The whisky crossed Scotland's borders and made it to England, where it got the royal seal of approval—paving its way to success throughout the country and the entire world.

Eventually, Chivas and Stewart's business partnership dissolved, and James brought in his brother John as a partner. The two of them changed the name of the store to Chivas Brothers and even opened a new branch, which was run by James' son, Alexander.

James died in 1886, and shortly afterward, Alexander—his son and heir—died as well. As John Chivas had also died years earlier, the store was transferred to two employees: Alexander Smith and Charles Howard. The two of them quickly developed a new superior-quality whisky blend, in which the youngest malt whisky component had been aged 12 years. They called the new blend Chivas Regal.

Chivas Regal 12 contains 35 different ingredients. The high-quality malt whisky at the heart of the Chivas blend is Strathisla, which is distilled in the town of Keith in the Speyside region in the north of Scotland. Strathisla, established in 1798, is listed as the oldest distillery in Speyside. The Chivas brothers purchased it, and today it is used mostly for producing Chivas.

In 2001 the drinks conglomerate Pernod Ricard purchased Chivas, which is currently one of the firm's most important strategic brands. Chivas Regal is the second-best-selling premium scotch in the world, and its sales are continuing to increase, especially in Europe and in Asia, and even in Israel, where it is very popular at event halls.

Charles Howard

Whisky-based cocktails have to strike the right balance between heavy alcohol that is soothing and warm, and other, lighter ingredients. Chivas Regal, a premium brand of blended whisky, with pleasant aromas of fruit and honey, provides a nice complexity without overpowering the cocktail.

Rob Roy

This cocktail is named after Robert Roy MacGregor (1671–1734), a Scottish folk hero. Also referred to as the Scottish Robin Hood, MacGregor devoted his life to defending the Highland way of life. Rob Roy joined the fight to support the king of Scotland, King James II of the House of Stuart, whose throne was being taken over by the king of England, William of Orange. MacGregor also became famous as a skilled whisky smuggler.

The Rob Roy cocktail was created about 150 years after the death of its namesake. The name was actually inspired by an operetta written about Rob Roy, rather than the man himself. Rob Roy MacGregor was nicknamed "Red MacGregor", because of his red hair, which is similar in color to the drink.

What you need (for one cocktail glass)	What to do
50 ml whisky 25 ml red vermouth A dash of Angostura bitters Ice Cherry and an orange peel twist for garnish	Fill the glass with ice. Combine the ingredients in a shaker with ice and stir gently with a spoon. Remove the ice from the glass and strain the cocktail into the glass. Garnish with the cherry and the orange peel twist.

Angostura bitters: An alcoholic mixture that is used to add a bitter and aromatic flavor to cocktails.

Rusty Nail

According to some legends, the origin of the name "Rusty Nail" can be traced back to the 1940s to a Scottish town called Kilmarnock. In the village lived a tough old man named John Rasdale, who liked to drown his sorrows in whisky but couldn't always afford to do so. So he decided to make his own, which he aged as required in an oak barrel that he'd made with his own two hands.

When the townspeople tasted his new whisky, which had a somewhat rusty flavor, they grimaced. John, who didn't want to lose the money he'd put in, added some Drambuie (Scottish honey liqueur) to the whiskey to improve the flavor. When the whisky in the barrel had all been drunk, the novice distiller realized that, when building the barrel, he had forgotten a rusty nail inside.

What you need
(for one lowball glass)

60 ml whisky
30 ml Drambuie
2 ice cubes
A slice of lemon for garnish

What to do

Pour the ingredients into a glass with ice and stir gently. Garnish with the lemon slice.

DISTILLING THE CONCEPTS | A BRIEF GLOSSARY OF DISTILLATION TERMS

Distillation   Distillation of alcoholic spirits is an age-old process. The technique was first used in China approximately three millennia BCE for the purpose of producing medicines and perfumes. People began to distill alcoholic beverages out of a desire to produce drinks with higher alcohol content compared with that of beverages made from fermented fruit. The spirit produced through distillation was called eau de vie, which means "water of life" in French. The distillation process eliminates components that might negatively affect the smell, the taste, or the texture of the spirit.

Batch distillation   This is the traditional method of distilling alcohol, and it is still commonly used to make high-quality beverages such as whisky, Cognac, and other aged spirits. The distillation takes place in copper stills, which are essentially large pots with long, curved necks. The liquid is heated up in the pot, and the alcohol vapor travels through the neck and condenses further down into a liquid with smaller volume, but with a higher alcohol concentration. Batch distillation preserves the original flavor of the fruit or the grain from which the spirit is produced, and beverages distilled in this way are typically of higher quality compared with those produced using newer techniques. However, the batch distillation process takes a long time and is also costly, as a great deal of liquid is lost in the production process.

Continuous distillation   This modern distillation method is cheaper than the traditional batch distillation method. The invention of continuous distillation marked the beginning of a new era of commercial alcohol production. In continuous distillation, the liquid goes through a system of containers and pipes, in which the evaporation and condensation processes occur much more quickly than they do in batch distillation. The advantage of continuous distillation is the high speed and the continuity, which enable the distiller

"Distillation", engraving by Stradano, 1550

American patent for a still, between 1836 and 1849

to achieve high concentrations of alcohol at lower cost (compared with the batch distillation method). The disadvantage is that you lose some of the flavor and color of the original version; the liquid that is produced is neutral and clear. The resultant beverage is often considered to be of lower quality compared with batch-distilled spirits.

Double distillation   To achieve very high alcohol concentrations when using pot stills, it is necessary to distill the spirit twice, in a process called double distillation. In the first round of distillation, assuming you begin with a spirit with alcohol concentration of about 10%, you can produce a spirit with an alcohol concentration of 25%. In the second round of distillation, you can get the alcohol concentration up to 75%. You then dilute the spirit with water until you achieve the ideal alcohol concentration.

Triple distillation   This process produces a spirit that is smooth, soft, and pleasant, and that goes down easy.

JOHNNIE WALKER

If you had to choose just one whisky out of Scotland's vast repertoire, Johnnie Walker Black Label would probably be the one to pick. Despite the "malt whisky revolution" that's taken place all over the world, and the abundance of different types of blended whisky, there aren't many whiskies that measure up to Johnnie in terms of complexity. This whisky is the yardstick against which all others should be compared. And to quote Jim Murray, who wrote the aptly-named *Whisky Bible*, the most comprehensive whisky guide in the world, "Black Label is the Savoy, the Everest of deluxe whiskies."

Johnnie has been "walking" for more than 200 years now. The original Johnnie Walker was born in 1805 to a family of farmers in the Scottish Highlands. When Johnnie was 14 his father died and the family farm was sold, and eventually the young man opened a small grocery in a nearby mining town. The shop thrived and, among other things, carried whisky. During that same period only malt whisky was being produced, much of it of dubious quality. Johnnie decided to try mixing several different malt whiskies into a single high-quality beverage. Over time, he became the leading malt mixer in the field. His clientele expanded and sales flourished. After Johnnie died, his son Alexander took over. Alexander had learned the secrets of mixing from his father, and in just six years he managed to produce his own blend and to market it to his customers. In 1870 Alexander Walker produced Johnnie Walker's distinctive square-shaped bottle and decorated it with the black label we all know today. By 1920 his whisky had reached 120 countries.

Alexander Walker's two sons also got involved in the family business. In 1906 the brothers began to produce a new and powerful whisky, the popular

Johnnie Walker Red Label, and they dedicated it to their father. Red Label became the best-sold brand of blended whisky worldwide. The whisky is composed of products from more than 35 different distilleries, and the most prominent malts in the blend are Cardhu, which gives the whisky a sweet, malty flavor, and Talisker, which contributes hints of smokiness and pepper.

In 1908 the Walker brothers decided that they needed a logo. They met with a well-known cartoonist, Tom Browne, and in that meeting one of the most famous logos of the alcohol world was born. The three men sat down for lunch, during which they had quite a lot to drink. The illustrator drew a sketch on the back of the menu in front of him: a picture of a "striding man", a British gentleman walking, and the portrait of Johnnie Walker as we know him today, and he added the tagline: "Born in 1820 and still going strong." Since then, the logo has been modified several times, such that the man walks in a different direction or wears different clothes. Where has he been walking for all these years? All the way to the bank, most likely.

JOHNNIE WALKER... AND A LOT OF IT

It was a busy Thursday evening, a day when many regulars liked to come by our bar. L. showed up, a beloved regular who would only drink the really hard stuff. Her eyes locked on a nice whisky that wasn't too expensive, a sign that a long night of drinking was about to begin. I poured her a glass, and then poured one for myself. We raised our glasses to the old sailor's proverb, "May we never drink seawater," and the whisky went down smooth.

The bar was crowded, but the regulars gladly made room for her. Even before drinking her hard stuff, L. was typically a riot, overflowing with great one-liners, and everyone wanted to be near her when it happened. But that night L. wasn't delivering the goods. She was lost in thought, staring into her glass in silence. It wasn't like her. The guys, in an unusual display of tact, didn't bug her about it, but were hoping things would improve later on, once she'd had a few rounds.

Out of the corner of my eye I noticed an unfamiliar male form, entering the pub with a confident spring in his step. He shot a quick, seemingly significant glance at L., but it seemed she'd decided that her drink would be her only date for the night. The long-legged waitress made her way through the crowd to take his order. She came back to me with a clear directive: "Johnnie Walker... and a lot of it." I poured some Johnnie Walker in the amount that is universally agreed upon as "a lot", which happens to be the exact same amount that I always pour into a serving of whisky, and I forgot about the guy before the waitress had even disappeared with the glass. Just before I forgot, I checked how much Johnnie Walker we had left on the bottom shelf, because I had a feeling we'd need it.

The pub was packed, but I couldn't help but notice that with every round of "Johnnie Walker... and a lot of it", the expressions on the faces of all the women in the guy's immediate vicinity grew darker. He was acting like a cock-of-the-walk, confident that his presence in the chicken coop was for the sole purpose of satisfying all the chicks. I kept an eye on him to see if intervention was needed, but it seemed like everyone was doing OK without my help.

It was late, and it was already technically Friday, and little by little the last of the customers began to go home, some to their own homes, some to someone else's. Johnnie was wandering the pub, and I noticed that his step was not as light and confident as it had been when he'd first come in. My friend L. was still sitting at the bar, and he ogled her with the universal drunken gaze, completely convinced of his charm and with no doubt in his mind that she would leap willingly into his arms. L., who was known for being assertive, tried to brush him aside, but even she was unsuccessful. I summoned my professional authority and spoke to the jerk sternly, informing him that we were closing and that he must leave immediately, and that I hoped he would do so willingly, otherwise I would have no choice but to call the cops. He paid and stumbled out.

I was cleaning up and organizing the bar for the day that was already dawning outside. L. paid her bill with relief. When she got up to say thanks and goodbye, I told her to wait. "Let's leave together," I said, "because I have a feeling that Johnnie won't give up so easily, he's probably waiting outside." After a little while we both went outside together. As I was locking the door I heard a suspicious rustling in the bushes by the pub. He was there, just as I'd thought.

L. and I looked deep into each other's eyes, both of us thinking the same thing. We started walking toward the parking lot, holding each other so as to send an unambiguous message. We stopped for one long minute and locked our lips in a long, sensual kiss, one that would make it clear to anyone watching that these were two people in a serious relationship. From the bushes we heard one loud, final crash. With satisfied smiles, we went our separate ways.

Though it's customary to drink whisky neat or on the rocks, the beverage can be great in cocktails, contributing a unique flavor and complexity. Whisky cocktails have many different flavors, ranging from harsh and smoky to fruity. Sometimes they have a light sweetness, and sometimes they are dry. Most whisky cocktails incorporate blended whisky, which is usually lighter and more accessible than single-malt whisky. Johnnie Walker, the best-selling whisky in the world, has a powerful and highly recognizable flavor, and it makes a special addition to any cocktail.

The Chancellor

Scotch has a somewhat stubborn personality and isn't always well-suited to cocktails. The Chancellor cocktail is an exception. For centuries, to make their whisky go down a little easier, people mixed it with ice and water or soda water. The Chancellor is a classic, pleasant cocktail that takes this idea a step further. It's a historical cocktail, a cousin of the Rob Roy and of the American Manhattan.

The origins of the Chancellor are somewhat murky and mysterious; it's hard to find trustworthy documentation of its creation. One unsourced claim is that it was born in the dining hall of a Scottish college, and was named after the chancellor of the university.

What you need
(for one cocktail glass)

40 ml whisky
20 ml ruby port wine (young
   port wine)
10 ml dry white vermouth
A drizzle of Angostura bitters
   (preferably orange flavored)
A lemon peel twist for garnish

What to do

Fill the glass with ice. Stir all the ingredients together in a shaker filled with ice. Remove the ice from the glass and strain the cocktail into the glass. Garnish with the lemon twist.

John Collins

Most classic cocktails have weird stories to go along with them. Some of them are about famous bars, and some of them are about people, real or imagined or something in between. John Collins' story is an extreme example of "something in between." The name John Collins belongs to someone completely real, the headwaiter at the bar of a hotel called Limmer's Old House, a popular place in London in the 1800s. Completely unrelatedly, in 1874 some newspapers on the East Coast of the US began to print stories about a mysterious fictional character named Tom Collins, and the name was on everyone's lips. "Have you seen Tom Collins?" and "Tom Collins was talking about you" were part of English slang until the end of the 19th century.

The Tom Collins phenomenon soon led to the invention of a cocktail called Tom Collins, whose main ingredient was gin. Eventually, "Collins" became a general name for any cocktail made of an alcoholic beverage mixed with sugar, lemon, and soda. The first two cocktails in the series were Tom Collins, based on gin, and John Collins, named after that same headwaiter in London, which was based on whisky. Later, new Collins drinks were invented, based on vodka and tequila.

What you need
(for one highball glass)

60 ml whisky
30 ml lemon juice
10 ml simple syrup (sugar water with
   a ratio of 1 part sugar to 1
   part water)
A drizzle of Angostura bitters
Soda water
Ice
A cherry and a lemon or orange slice
   for garnish

What to do

Fill the glass with ice. Combine all ingredients, except the soda water, in a shaker with ice, and shake. Strain the cocktail into the glass and add soda up to the rim of the glass. Garnish with the cherry and lemon or orange slice.

Winston Churchill (1874–1965) was a heavy drinker. He could start the morning off with a glass of white wine and wash it down with a glass of Johnnie Walker Black mixed with water. He was very attached to his "Johnnie," which, he claimed, gave him a feeling of peace and tranquility. When one of his fellow party members accused him of being "disgustingly drunk," he answered: "My dear, you are ugly, and what's more, you are disgustingly ugly. But tomorrow I shall be sober and you will still be disgustingly ugly." And to another woman, who told him: "Winston, if I were your wife, I would put poison in your coffee," Churchill replied: "Nancy, if I were your husband, I would drink it."

A doctor who treated Churchill after an accident said that he needed at least a third of a bottle of liquor per day in order to function, and ordered that Churchill be given drinks during mealtimes. It seems that Churchill never recovered from his ailment, and different types of alcohol flowed freely at all his meals, including Champagne, wine and port, and Cognac at the end. According to some estimates, he would drink two bottles of brandy per day. Still, Churchill lived until the age of 91, happy and generally healthy, and, as you know, he had a successful career. When asked about his age one day, he replied: "I leave when the pub closes."

Winston Churchill

"There is no bad whiskey.
There are only some whiskeys
that aren't as good as others."

Raymond Chandler,
American mystery writer.

JAMESON

If you've ever been to Ireland, the land of fairies, elves and leprechauns, you'll never forget it. The green landscapes are breathtaking and have a fairy-tale charm, an air of simplicity and joy. True, it rains there most of the time, but there's an old Irish proverb that says, "It never rains in a pub." And indeed, the most common family outing on the Emerald Isle is to the local pub, the one where they play a lot of music and serve a lot of beer, mainly Guinness, and, of course, whiskey (in Ireland, it's spelled with an "e").

Whiskey lovers will immediately feel at home in Ireland, and any pub you visit is likely to have a nice selection of liquor in which Irish whiskey features prominently. Jameson is one Irish brand that's famous all over the world; in fact, it may be the highest-sold Irish whiskey anywhere. It's smooth and pleasant, a great starter drink for people who are just beginning to discover the world of whiskey, and connoisseurs can still appreciate it, especially the longer-aged varieties.

The Scots and the Irish have long disputed the true birthplace of whisky (or whiskey). The first documented mention of whiskey was actually in Ireland, where whiskey was distilled by monks. In a manuscript from the year 1405, which is housed at Oxford University, an Irish doctor named Gadsden referred to old texts mentioning the use of whiskey (grain spirit) as a medicine against paralysis of the tongue. The first mention of Scotch whisky appears in a text from 1496, though the Scots claim that at that point the beverage had already been in use for centuries.

In the year 1780 John Jameson, a passionate businessman, established his distillery on Bow Street in Dublin, on the northern bank of the Liffey.

He had come from a courageous family known for pursuing and catching pirates, and the Jameson family motto was "Sine Metu", "without fear." John Jameson married a daughter of Scottish distillers. In Scotland he learned the secrets of distilling whisky and then emigrated from Scotland to Dublin. His eldest son married the daughter of the previous owner of the distillery on Bow Street, which John bought several years later.

The Jameson family became one of the largest whiskey-producing families in Ireland. John quickly perfected his distillation craft, and his high-quality whiskey became widely renowned. The distillery thrived in Ireland for many years, and around the beginning of the 20th century Jameson's whiskey began to be sold all over the world. By the end of the 19th century the Jameson distillery had grown so much that it had 300 workers producing about a million liters of whiskey per year.

During the following years the Irish alcohol industry suffered several crippling blows: The phylloxera epidemic, which wiped out vineyards all over the world and caused the brandy industry to shut down completely, helped the Scottish whisky industry to establish itself in the world, and it ultimately displaced Irish whiskey, whose production began to shrink. Things only got worse in the 1920s, with Prohibition in the US, as well as Ireland's trade war with the UK, from which Ireland had seceded. By the 1960s it had become clear to the Irish that the only way to break the vicious cycle was for distilleries to unite and work together. In 1966, the four largest Irish distilleries, with Jameson's distillery at their head, merged to create the Irish Distillers group. This move enabled the Irish whiskey industry to reconquer the global market. In 1988 the alcohol giant Pernod Ricard purchased the Irish Distillers and began to market the group's products, with a strong emphasis on Jameson. Nowadays, Jameson whiskey is sold in more than 120 countries. Much of its popularity can be attributed to the various sporting events that the brand sponsors—horse races and golf in Ireland, yacht races in the US, and more. In 1996 Jameson was recognized as the fastest-growing drink brand, when it reached sales levels of one million cases per year.

Jameson Distillery, Dublin, the 19ᵗʰ century

Jameson is the highest-sold Irish whiskey in the world. Marketed in more than 120 countries and selling more than 20 million bottles per year, it is considered to be one of the fastest-growing brands in the alcohol industry worldwide. Jameson's triple distillation process gives it a soft and velvety feel, and the whiskey is aged in barrels that once contained Spanish sherry, giving it a soft and fruity flavor that is refined and slightly sweet. Jameson is great for amateur whiskey drinkers and works well in cocktails, which is probably why it is considered to be a bartender's whiskey.

It is customary to drink Jameson with a lot of ice, or mixed with water, the way the Irish do. In recent years Irish Jameson drinkers have begun to add ginger ale or ginger beer to the drink, creating a sweet and pleasant cocktail.

The Presbyterian

In recent years we're seeing more and more whiskey cocktails in chi-chi bars all over the world. These cocktails are usually based on Irish whiskey, because of its soft and pleasant flavor. The most common cocktail is the simple combination of whiskey and ginger ale.

The Presbyterian is a classic cocktail with many variations, despite containing only three ingredients. Some use ginger ale, and others use Sprite or other lemon-lime mixers. The only constant is the whiskey.

**What you need
(for one highball glass)**

60 ml whiskey
Soda water
Ginger ale or ginger beer
Ice
A slice of lime for garnish

What to do

Put ice in the glass and pour in the whiskey. Add equal amounts of soda water and ginger ale up to the rim of the glass. Garnish with the slice of lime.

Irish Coffee

As strange as it might seem to call Irish coffee a cocktail, in Ireland this whiskey-containing beverage is almost as popular as the national beer, Guinness. It's hard to find an Irishman or woman who doesn't top off dinner with a steaming mug of sweet Irish coffee.

Irish coffee was first created in 1942 by an Irish chef named Joe Sheridan, the manager of a restaurant at an airport in Ireland. It was a very stormy night, and a plane that had taken off for New York was forced to return to the airport. Sheridan made a hot, comforting beverage for all the passengers on the plane: coffee mixed with whiskey and cream. One of the American passengers asked the chef if it was Brazilian coffee. "No, it's Irish coffee," said the chef, and coined the name of the beverage. Irish coffee became a hit at the airport.

In 1952 a travel writer brought the recipe to the US and caught the attention of a bartender at the Buena Vista hotel bar in San Francisco. When the bartender tried to make the beverage, the cream sank to the bottom. So he went to Ireland to learn the recipe from Sheridan himself. Ultimately, the bartender offered Sheridan a job at the California hotel. To this day, you can get original Irish Coffee at the Buena Vista.

What you need
(for one mug)

90 ml hot coffee, strong and rich
45 ml whiskey
2 tsp brown sugar
30 ml whipped cream

What to do

Pour the coffee into the mug. Add sugar and stir. Add whiskey and stir again. Top the drink with the cream by pouring over the back of the spoon. Do not stir; drink the coffee through the cream.

The Irish make this drink using double cream.

THE IRISH ARE COMING

A group of Irish construction workers had come to work in the area, and because our pub was close to their hotel, they adopted us as their neighborhood watering hole, and didn't travel further to one of the Irish bars in the area. Quite an honor. They were great customers. They'd work from 7 a.m. until 7 p.m., and then at 7:20 they would be the first to show up at the pub. The older ones would arrive straight from the bus in their work clothes, unshaved and ready to drink. Only on Friday would they arrive clean-shaven, dressed in their very best. On Saturdays the pub would open at 11 a.m., and they would already be there, waiting outside. They'd stay until the end of the day, and eat lunch as well. The young ones would show up later. Not straight from work but after a two-hour nap, showered and in clean clothes. Both the younger ones and the older ones were cheerful and happy and would chat among themselves in English in an accent that I didn't always understand.

I, of course, would always nod and agree with whatever they were saying. When they talked about beer I could usually keep up—but less so when they talked about other things. Their accents were heavy, too northern or too southern. And they knew how to drink: They would down about 18 pints each in an evening, and some would have even more. And they had their own unique customs. For example, they would order in groups of three, like this: One person would order a round. When the beer was halfway done, the next person would order. And then when that beer was halfway done, the third would order, and so on.

They were all characters. A stereotypical redhead, a blond with pale skin, freckled guys and red-faced guys, older men with red noses. One would tell stories; he was full of them, having traveled all over the world. He would drink nonstop, and fairly quickly, and it didn't seem to have any effect on him. Some of the guys revealed that the man's work involved climbing up onto roofs, and everyone was always on the alert, because he'd fallen once before and had been badly injured. But here he was, doing his thing, bothered by nothing, not even by the platinum plates that had been implanted in his body. And then there was the one who would always collapse at the end of the evening, flat on the floor. A few of his friends would go to him, help him up and take him home.

The workers were generally polite and nice all evening long, except for one who, it was told, sometimes became violent when he drank, and everyone was careful not to make him angry. He was always very friendly to me, and I never saw him lose control, but they warned me that there were a lot of stories about him, and his friends would tell those stories only before he arrived and after he left.

On St. Patrick's Day we wanted to do something nice for them: We decorated the pub in green, in keeping with Irish custom. And they made an effort for us too; they invited lots of British and Irish friends that they'd met in Israel. The place was packed beyond capacity, and in honor of the holiday everyone was drinking Guinness and shots of Jameson. One of the older ones, whom they called the Mayor (it turned out he'd once been the mayor of a small town), got up to sing. A group of musicians joined him, with a flute, an Irish drum, strange string instruments, and more, and he began to sing, an endless tune. A story about Mary, a girl who would ring-ring-ring, and her fellow, who had a ring-ring-ring, and she did this and that and he went here and there, and they went back and forth and here and there, and on and on and on. *How is he remembering all the words?* I wondered to myself. *Is he making them up as he goes along?* But all the young men were singing and dancing along with him, red-faced with alcohol, happiness, and the holiday spirit.

Around midnight the older ones ordered a last round of Irish coffee—hot coffee with Irish whiskey and cream on top—and left the bar to make room for the younger ones. The younger ones drank until four, five, and even six in the morning. Finally, they returned to their hotel, changed into their work clothes, and then went out to wait for the 6:30 bus that would take them to work.

"I love to sing, and I love to drink
scotch. Most people would rather
hear me drink scotch."

George Burns,
American comedian and entertainer

AMERICAN WHISKEY

American whiskey is very popular among novice whiskey drinkers, mainly because it is soft and sweet, and easier to drink compared with its European counterparts. American whiskey is known for its sweet fruitiness, with a strong wood finish and buttery caramel flavors. And there's a story behind those flavors.

Most whiskey produced in the US today is bourbon, which the US Congress declared in 1964 as a drink that would be a "distinctive product of the United States." At the beginning of the 19th century, Thomas Jefferson, the third president of the young United States, offered land in the south to the new settlers who were coming in. Most of the settlers were immigrants from Scotland and Ireland who were trying to escape poverty and hunger in their countries of origin. The settlers discovered that they could grow corn and rye, and they filled the land with those crops and tried to sell them. But it was very complex to transport their harvests, and the farmers had to search for new ways to make money from their crops. And then some people had the idea of converting the corn and rye into whiskey. It turns out that it's easier for a horse to pull casks of whiskey than to carry large amounts of corn or flour. And even more importantly, unlike the raw agricultural products, which spoiled quickly in transport, whiskey only benefited from long journeys, as it continued to age and improve. Another advantage was that the price of whiskey was stable, and you could always find someone to buy it.

In Maryland and in Pennsylvania distillers made whiskey out of rye, whereas in Virginia and in Kentucky they made it out of corn. In the late 18th century George Washington (who, ironically, was a distiller himself) had imposed heavy taxes on whiskey distillers. The distillers rebelled and traveled south to regions in Kentucky and Tennessee that had not yet been settled. But ultimately, they all had to pay the taxes.

One of the pioneers who migrated south during this time was a Baptist preacher named Elijah Craig, who is considered to be one of the inventors of bourbon. Craig, who came from Virginia, settled in Kentucky in 1786. After about three years of experimentation, he successfully distilled whiskey from corn. Historians claim that the idea originated from a corn-based Native American beverage.

The preacher set up a distillery in Georgetown and produced whiskey from a blend of corn, barley, and rye. He is also credited as being the first to age whiskey in burnt oak barrels. Some people claim that the barrel he used to age whiskey in was originally a fish barrel, and that to get rid of the smell of fish Craig charred the wood with fire. It turns out that the charring had significant effects on the final product: It gave the whiskey a dark color, a soft flavor, and a pleasant, vanilla-like sweetness. Craig sent his new whiskey to New Orleans and immediately got another order for "Bourbon whiskey", "Bourbon" being the name of the county he lived in, and the word that was printed on the barrels before they were sent down the river. Elijah Craig became famous all over the US, until in 1795 he was caught by federal agents and was charged with producing whiskey without a license. He was sentenced to a very large fine, and he disappeared. By that point, though, American bourbon had already taken off.

Distilleries started popping up like mushrooms all over the US and the whiskey flowed like water, until 1919, when the Prohibition Act spoiled all the fun. In fact, as early as the 19th century, a movement had already emerged in the US to protest alcohol consumption. Religious rules against drinking on the one hand and medical evidence of the dangers of alcoholism on the other caused a great deal of concern, especially in the face of massive waves of immigration that had brought new drinking customs along with

them, increasing alcohol consumption in the US. The low prices of alcoholic beverages and their poor quality made the problems associated with alcohol even worse. The Prohibition Act, which forbade the production, import, export, purchase, transport, and sale of alcohol throughout the entire US, was legislated in 1919 and took effect a year later, in January 1920.

But the law was too much for the public to bear. It triggered a large wave of illegal activity, especially underground distillation and smuggling of alcohol. The Mafia and crime underworld thrived in these years, operating in the black market and selling alcohol to whomever was willing to pay for it. An entire industry of illegal business began to flourish all over the US. An underground network of pubs called speakeasies opened up, and people flocked to them not only to purchase alcohol but also to enjoy musical and burlesque performances. Alcoholic beverages were smuggled in from Canada, Mexico, Cuba, and other neighbors, and illegal distillers ("moonshiners") began to operate covertly in every corner of the country. They produced beverages under no sanitary supervision whatsoever, and their products sent many a drinker to a better place.

The authorities ultimately realized that the draconian laws weren't working and that they were helpless to quash the smuggling and to prevent alcoholic beverages from being sold. In 1933 the Prohibition Act was repealed, and alcohol could once again be sold legally.

WHAT'S THE DIFFERENCE BETWEEN BOURBON, TENNESSEE WHISKEY AND RYE?

Bourbon   According to US law, to be legally eligible to be called "bourbon", a spirit must contain at least 51% corn in the mash of grains used to distill it, its alcohol content should be no more than 80%, and it must be aged in new oak barrels for at least two years. Because cornstarch cannot be converted into sugar on its own without enzymes, bourbon always contains a small amount of germinated barley (malt) to trigger the fermentation process. The Scots and the Irish often say that American bourbon is not real whiskey, because it is not distilled from barley but rather from aged corn. American bourbon is known for its sweet fruity flavors and strong aroma of wood. Because of its sweet flavor it is quite easy on the palate.

Tennessee whiskey   The process of producing Tennessee whiskey is similar to the process of producing bourbon, but Tennessee whiskey has to be made in the state of Tennessee. After distillation, it is not transferred directly to a barrel like other American whiskeys, but instead has to be filtered for 12 days through charcoal filters made of maple wood. The filtration process is called the Lincoln County Process, and it is patented and trademarked. The two distilleries best known for producing Tennessee whiskey are Jack Daniels and George Dickel. Tennessee whiskey is clean, smooth, refined, and slightly sweet.

Rye whiskey   To be sold as such, rye whiskey must meet a few criteria. The grain mixture from which it is distilled has to contain at least 51% rye, and its alcohol concentration cannot exceed 80%. It has to be aged in new barrels made of charred American oak. After the Prohibition era there weren't many rye whiskey producers left, and nowadays rye whiskey is less popular than bourbon.

Why is it sometimes spelled "whisky" and sometimes "whiskey"?
The Scots spell it "whisky" and the Americans and Irish spell it
"whiskey." Until the 1870s, all whisky producers used the Scottish
spelling, "whisky." But around that time, Scotch whisky began to
get a bad reputation, because most brands were distilled using
continuous distillation, and American and Irish distillers added the
letter "e" to distinguish their own products.

"George Washington" (detail), Gilbert Stuart, 1803

Old Fashioned

The Old Fashioned cocktail is usually served in a glass that bears its name, the Old Fashioned glass. According to legend, this cocktail first appeared in the 19th century, in a gentlemen's club in Louisville, Kentucky. The recipe was invented by the club's bartender as an homage to Col. James E. Pepper, a well-known whiskey distiller. From there the word spread to the Waldorf Astoria hotel in New York, which had a major influence on the cocktail world. The drink was very popular during the 1960s and then faded away, until the arrival of *Mad Men*'s Don Draper, whose love for the cocktail brought it back into fashion.

In the US some people believe that the classic Old Fashioned was the first cocktail made in America.

What you need
(for one lowball glass)

60 ml whiskey
1 tsp or 1 cube of brown sugar
1 orange slice
1 tsp water
A drizzle of Angostura bitters
Ice
A cherry for garnish

What to do

Muddle the sugar and orange in the glass. Add the water and Angostura bitters and stir. Add ice. Pour in whiskey and stir well. Garnish with the cherry.

Some people prefer to muddle the cherry together with the orange and sugar. Some add lemon zest.

Manhattan

This cocktail is a true classic. Like the people who live in Manhattan, it is sophisticated, urban, and worldly. According to legend, this cocktail was invented by a bartender in New York in 1874 in a club called Manhattan. The cocktail was made for a party hosted by Lady Randolph Churchill (Winston Churchill's American-born mother) in honor of the New York governor's reelection. Some people claim that the cocktail was invented in honor of Lady Churchill herself when she was visiting New York.

What you need
(for one martini glass)

60 ml whiskey
30 ml red vermouth
A drizzle of Angostura bitters
A cherry for garnish

What to do

Fill the glass with ice. Combine all the ingredients in a shaker with ice and stir with a long spoon. Remove the ice from the glass and strain the cocktail into the glass. Garnish with the cherry.

Mint Julep

The julep is a very old drink. In Arabic it was called *julab*, meaning rose water, and was prepared with no alcohol, with water and with rose petals. In the Middle East the rose petals were ultimately replaced with mint. In Latin the word is *julapium*, and the most common term, julep, comes from French. The drink has as many variations as it has names, with different types of alcohol.

Two US states claim to have invented the contemporary mint julep: Georgia and Virginia. But Kentucky is the state that made it famous. That's because the mint julep is the official cocktail of the famous horse race, the Kentucky Derby, which is held every year in Louisville, Kentucky on the first Saturday in May. According to some estimates, more than 80,000 cups of mint julep are poured every year during the Derby weekend.

Many horseracing fans collect Kentucky Derby souvenir glasses, called tumblers. These are the glasses that mint julep is traditionally served in at the Derby; they are colored silver and are printed with the name of the winning horse and the date of its victory. The winner gets a dozen commemorative glasses.

**What you need
(for one highball glass)**

60 ml whiskey
1 handful of fresh mint leaves
2 sugar cubes or 2 tsp sugar
Crushed ice

What to do

Muddle the mint and the sugar in the glass. Add the whiskey and then fill the glass with ice. Stir well and garnish with more mint.

COGNAC

ℬ

Grapes
one of the components of Cognac

THE DRINK THAT WAS BORN BY MISTAKE

Some people believe that the concept of distilling wine into brandy began with a mistake: A Dutch captain was transporting wine in the hold of his ship, and wanted to save space. He decided to distill the wine, thinking that if he later diluted the spirit with water, it would turn back into wine. The seaman quickly realized his mistake, but the result of the happy accident was a new beverage that the Dutch called *brandewijn*, meaning "burnt wine", a precursor of the word "brandy."

Even if that story is only a myth—which seems likely considering that wine distillation is the oldest form of distillation known to man—there is definitely a connection between Dutch sailors and French Cognac. The root of this connection is actually in the salt trade, which was one of France's most significant sources of income during the Middle Ages. In those days, salt was worth as much as gold and was shipped to northern Europe, where it was hard to come by.

The Charente river in the Cognac region of western France was one of the sources from which sea salt was harvested, and it was one of the main shipping channels for salt, as the ports along the river were considered to be very well suited to ship traffic. And salt was not the only commodity produced in the region; wine was produced and sold there as well. The wine merchants in the area joined forces with the salt merchants and loaded their products onto the same ships that set sail for the north, mainly to Scandinavia and the Netherlands. Unfortunately, however, the quality of the wine tended to deteriorate significantly by the time it arrived at its destination. The problem was only solved when, at the end of the 16th century, the Dutch established distilleries in the Cognac region and began to distill their own brandy from the wine. They shipped the brandy in oak barrels, which led to the discovery (an accidental discovery, like so many important discoveries) that contact with wood greatly improved the spirit and added special new aromas and flavors.

Since then, aging in oak barrels has been an inseparable part of the brandy distillation process, and the longer a brandy is aged, the higher its quality. By the way, unlike wine, brandy does not continue to age after it is transferred to a bottle, and therefore the age of a brandy is the amount of time it has spent in the barrel. Cognac can be aged for between 2 and 100 years, according to the decision of the master blender.

Now is a good time to clarify that all Cognacs are brandy, but not every brandy is Cognac. Only brandy that has been distilled from wine produced in the Cognac region, where there are optimal growing conditions for the grape varieties that presumably produce the highest-quality brandy, can legally be called by that name. Cognac is considered to be a premium beverage all over the world, and it is France's highest-earning export, bringing in more revenue than any other product. In fact, the French market for Cognac is quite small, and more than 90% of the Cognac that France produces is made for export to more than 165 countries all over the world. About half is sold in Europe, and the other half is divided between the US and Asia, where the market for Cognac has grown in recent years, particularly in East Asia.

Cognac is a rich and aromatic beverage, fruity with a full and generous body. A sip of the stuff sends a warm, pleasant feeling through your mouth, coupled with a light sweetness and hints of dark chocolate, nuts, and even citrus. It's nice to drink it neat at room temperature, but it also makes a great addition to prestigious cocktails.

RÉMY MARTIN

Rémy Martin is the best-known Cognac in the world. It is named after a winemaker who was born in 1695 in a small town in the Cognac region and who is credited with producing some of France's finest wines during the 18th century. In the year 1724, Rémy Martin bought several excellent vineyards in Cognac and established a small brandy distillery. He passed his passion on to four generations, who continued to distill the beverage and who named their company after him.

Every bottle of Rémy Martin bears the words "Fine Champagne Cognac." These words mean that 100% of the grapes used to make the beverage come from the two finest growing areas, or *crus*, in the Cognac region: Grande Champagne and Petite Champagne. It is important to note that Grande Champagne and Petite Champagne have no relation to the province of Champagne, which is famous for producing sparkling wine (that Champagne is in the northeast of France).

Another important fact about Cognac is that its bottles are marked according to how long the beverage inside them has been aged, with the letters VSOP, VS, or XO (see the next page for an explanation of what each notation means). Rémy Martin VSOP, which was first produced in 1927 and is the basic Cognac sold by the company, is the best-selling Cognac in the VSOP category. The person who decides how long a batch of Cognac will be aged is the master blender. For many years now, a woman named Pierrette Trichet has been the person responsible for the giant casks of Cognac at Rémy Martin. Each cask contains a large batch of cognac, and the contents of a single cask can be worth as much as 600 thousand Euros! For every barrel that is sold, there are eight more that are still undergoing the aging process.

WHAT ARE THOSE LETTERS ON THE LABEL?

V.S: VERY SPECIAL

VS Cognac has been aged for at least two-and-a-half years in the barrel. More prestigious distilleries tend to age this Cognac for about five years.

V.S.O.P: VERY SUPERIOR OLD PALE

VSOP Cognac is aged for at least four years in the barrel, and more prestigious distilleries age it for at least seven years.

X.O: EXTRA OLD

XO Cognac must be aged for at least six years in the barrel. Elite distillers age it for at least 12, and up to 20 years.

PRESTIGE

Most Cognac distillers have a Prestige label, which is aged longer than other labels. It's not always possible to know the exact age of a Prestige Cognac, but it can range between 40 and 100 years.

Rémy Martin estate

FROM GENTLEMEN TO RAPPERS

The alcohol world is generally young, innovative, and surprising. Cognac has always been something of an exception: For years it was considered to be dignified, mature, and stable, to be consumed by the fireplace at the end of a hearty meal. In recent years, however, Cognac has taken a leap into night life. All of a sudden, people are drinking it with ice, ginger ale, tonic, and cranberry juice—mixes that, in the past, would have drawn the ire of distillers and bartenders alike.

Nowadays, we're seeing ad campaigns for Cognac aimed at young people who like to party. At the same time, Cognac has become associated with several major rappers, who use it to convey their status and prestige. The first rapper to mention Cognac in a song was P. Diddy in his 2001 hit "Pass the Courvoisier", which triggered a spike in Cognac consumption in the US. Many other rappers followed suit, and some of them have collaborated with venerable Cognac labels to help them market their products to young people.

"Always do sober what you said you'd do drunk. That will teach you to keep your mouth shut."

Ernest Hemingway

Sidecar

According to legend, the original recipe for the Sidecar was invented after World War I by Harry MacElhone of Harry's New York Bar in Paris. The cocktail was supposedly named after an eccentric military officer who was a regular at the bar and would be driven there in the sidecar of a motorcycle. Eventually, Harry wrote a book in which he refuted this story; he gave the credit to a man named McGarry, a popular bartender at the Buck's Club in London.

**What you need
(for one cocktail glass)**

60 ml Cognac
30 ml orange liqueur
30 ml fresh-squeezed lemon juice
Ice
Brown sugar

What to do

Fill the glass with ice. Combine all ingredients (except the sugar) in a shaker with ice and shake. Remove the ice from the glass. Dip the rim of the glass in the brown sugar and strain the cocktail into the glass.

Cognac Horse's Neck

The Horse's Neck is a brandy-based cocktail (in the US it is sometimes made with whiskey) with ginger ale and lemon. The cocktail originated in 1890 as a non-alcoholic beverage—just a mix of ginger ale, ice, and a lemon peel twist. Brandy was first added to the mix in 1910, to create a horse with a "kick." The non-alcoholic version of the drink continued to be served in New York until the 1960s, when it eventually faded away.

The Horse's Neck has been mentioned in many films, starting with *Caught in a Cabaret*, a 1914 silent film starring Charlie Chaplin, and in a 1935 film starring Fred Astaire. A 1950 film noir starring Humphrey Bogart featured the non-alcoholic version, and Ian Fleming, who was a fan of the cocktail himself, describes it in *Octopussy* as "the drunkard's drink."

The cocktail was also very popular in the officers' barracks of the Royal Navy during the 1960s, and it displaced the Pink Gin cocktail, which had previously been the officers' cocktail of choice.

What you need
(for one highball glass)

60 ml Cognac
Ginger ale
Ice
Lemon peel twist

What to do

Fill the glass with ice and position the lemon peel twist in the glass so that one edge of the twist is on the lip of the glass and the other edge is at the bottom of the glass, beneath the ice. Pour in the Cognac and add ginger ale up to the rim of the glass.

BRANDY IN THE HOLY LAND

In Israel, the conditions for growing grapes for brandy aren't as good as those in the Cognac region of France, but we still do quite well for ourselves. Brandy production in the region began as early as 1898, in the Carmel vineyards, where winemakers were faced with a surplus of white grapes and had to find something to do with them.

In 1930 the region's brandy distilling industry got a professional boost when a continuous-distillation tower was built in the city of Rishon Le-Zion. When the State of Israel was established in 1948, the Carmel Winery used some of the reparation funds received from the German government to purchase pot stills. The two brandy labels that it produced—777 and Extra Fine—became the first liquors to be commercially produced in the country. Later, additional wineries began to distill brandy as well, including Barkan (Stock 84), Segal (Grand 41), Binyamina (BBB), and Tishbi (Jonathan Tishbi).

In 1998 in the prestigious IWSC competition in London, two Israeli brands were awarded the coveted title of Best Brandy: Tishbi's brandy and Carmel's Brandy 100.

From The Drunkard's Song /
Nathan Alterman

One little drink, friends,
there's nothing quite like it!
A little tipple isn't very risky.
True, some people do get drunk from it,
But I... 'tis strange... never get tipsy.
See, drinking is an art, *ya habib*,
And we are artists: Me-and Mottel Ziv.

When we our first libation guzzle down
Dear Mottel cries that I'm his bestest chum
When we our second drinks together clink,
Kiss I my Mottel on his ruddy cheeks.
And when we toast our fiery drink the third,
We make our soulful singing voices heard!
But when we have our tipple number four-
A dozen cops are already at the door!
Five and six is dandy
An Englishman's a limey,
In German bottle's Buttel
And Mottel is just Muttel...
My friends, one little drink is just the stuff,
But however much you drink it's not enough.

Translated from the Hebrew by Oded Even-Or

Nathan Alterman and Tirza Atar at a café, c. 1960.
From the Alexander Penn Archives, Kipp Center, Tel Aviv University

Nathan Alterman, one of Israel's most respected poets and journalists, was known for his love of liquor. One famous story describes the poet sitting at Café Kassit, a popular hangout for bohemians and artistic types at the time. The waitress went up to Alterman and asked: "What can I get you, Mr. Alterman?" "What do you have?" the poet asked. "We have whisky, Cognac, wine, beer, vodka, arak, slivovitz, vishniak…" "Meideleh, I don't care what you order you bring it in," he replied.

THE WHEEL IS COME FULL CIRCLE

Reidel means "wheel" in Yiddish. This story completes a full circle. This is the story as told to Gadi Ramon of Zichron Yaakov by Mr. Pfeffen, a Zichron native, who, at the age of 77, was at peak strength: tan, muscular, and articulate, spouting stories and pearls of wisdom in Hebrew, Arabic, and Yiddish.

"When I was a kid here in Zichron, which was smaller then, and different, I used to tag along with the grown-ups who would gather together in the reidel. The reidel was Zichron's parliament, as it were. It was called that because of the way the group of farmers would stand in a circle (reidel means "wheel" in Yiddish) at the corner of the main street, where they would discuss the various pressing issues of the day.

"During one of those conversations, on a warm, sultry summer evening, a heated debate arose about whether the women of the town should be permitted to participate in these reidel gatherings, along with the men. Until then it had been taken for granted that the circle was intended for men only. After all, what could a woman possibly contribute to the critical decisions that were made there? Questions of how many cows would fit onto the new pasture that had recently been leased to the town by the generous Baron, or on which day it would be better to begin harvesting the grapes so that they would ferment better at the winery later on, and even arguments about when the first rain of the year would fall or when the first desert wind would blow in from the east or from the south—and so on and so forth. Never had more important topics been discussed.

"To make sure you comprehend the significance of the suggestion," Mr. Pfeffen continued, "allowing a woman to enter the reidel was the equivalent of the Satmar Rebbe giving permission to eat a pork chop on Yom Kippur.

"The idea of including women in the reidel had been proposed by a man named Mendel, who was married to one Zelda, a very opinionated woman with a booming voice, who would pitilessly tyrannize anyone in her immediate vicinity. Mendel himself was a little unusual in the group, because he had studied for a year and a half at a university in Bucharest, mostly biology. He didn't have a muscular and powerful physique like the other farmers, and he didn't have a thick bushy mustache, but he knew a thing or two about raising crops, and many would come to him to seek out his professional opinion.

"So as I was saying," continued Pfeffen, "the argument reached extraordinary volumes, and the shouts could be heard all the way to the edge of the town, where our friends Mendel and Zelda lived. The hour was getting late, the sun was setting, and the sound of cursing and swearing reached Zelda's ears. Zelda decided to make the brave and unprecedented decision to go to the reidel herself to find out why everyone was shouting and why her husband was taking so long to come home. As she approached the circle of sweaty men, who were completely engrossed in yelling and cursing at one another, she was shocked to see her own husband standing at the center, surrounded by the other farmers of the community, who were all fired up and spitting out every curse in the vocabulary at the time, in Hebrew, Arabic, and Yiddish.

"So Mendel himself was standing helpless at the center of the circle, and looking a little pale amid all the shouting and cursing, and he was trying to explain his position, but you couldn't hear his voice; you could only see his lips moving, as if he were trying, and failing, to convey some message. Then farmer Ivan took it one step further (Ivan wasn't his real name, but because he was the biggest and strongest bully in the village everyone was afraid of his powerful fists, and called him Ivan the Terrible), and he approached poor Mendel with his thick arm raised with unmistakable intentions.

"At this point, Zelda did two things, which would continue to be talked about for generations. To everyone's amazement, she broke into the circle of men,

rushed like a whirlwind at Ivan, and before any of the men could react to the presence of a woman in the very heart of the reidel, for the first time ever in our community, she raised her own hand and slapped Ivan right across the face. They say that the sound of that slap reverberated throughout the village, as loudly as the shouting that had preceded it."

Ramon says he is willing to swear that at this point in the story, Pfeffen's voice quivered, and his eyes grew misty. "Everyone fell silent," Pfeffen continued. "They were shocked. Zelda hooked her arm in her husband's and marched him out of the circle towards the house, as the stunned farmers looked on, silently clearing a path for them to pass through.

"And that," Pfeffen concluded his story, "was how two myths in our little village were shattered in just three seconds. A woman entered the reidel for the first time, and Ivan got slapped for the first time—and by a woman."

After a minute or two of silence, Gadi Ramon was feeling curious, and he asked Mr. Pfeffen if Zelda and Mendel had ever had children, and if so, where they were now.

"Of course they had children," the man answered humbly, "I am the only child of those two wonderful people, may they rest in peace."

Gadi Ramon wrote down Pfeffen's story, and it won a competition in honor of the 130th anniversary of Zichron Yaakov. In 1996, after he'd seen a thing or two as a ship captain in the merchant marine, Ramon decided to drop anchor and to open up a bar in the heart of Zichron Yaakov, in the exact same place where the local parliament used to meet 100 years earlier, and he called it by the reidel's name. I had the honor of working as a bartender at the Reidel for several years and to be part of it from the very beginning, during the good days and during the not-so-good days. I can still feel its pulse in my veins. I made many friends there, and many of the regulars at the pub became regulars in my life. Thank you all.

DIGESTIF

JÄGERMEISTER

9 |

A flower of the cinnamon plant
one of the components of Jägermeister

SOMETHING TO END WITH

A digestif is an alcoholic beverage that is consumed at the end of a meal. The word comes from French, and it means "something that helps with digestion." Digestifs are typically divided into two categories: The first is the functional digestif, a beverage that actually soothes the stomach and the digestive system. Most drinks in this category were used medicinally for digestion-related purposes at one time or another. The other category includes classic beverages that are served at the end of a meal as part of local tradition, regardless of their effect on digestion.

Both types of digestifs have high alcohol concentrations, which is appropriate given that after the stomach has been lined with a hearty meal, the body absorbs alcohol relatively slowly and is therefore more capable of dealing with high alcohol levels. There is even a lower risk of getting drunk, as compared with drinking on an empty stomach.

Sometime around the late 20th century, after many years in which digestifs was considered the domain of the elderly, they became fashionable among younger people, mainly because of their high alcohol content and their unique bitter-medicinal flavor. One drink that can be credited for the revival of the digestif is the Jägermeister, one of the most prominent digestifs in the world. Jägermeister is the flagship product of Germany's liquor industry, and it is Europe's top exported beverage. Until the end of the 20th century, digestifs tended to be popular in countries in which food has an important role, and where the point of drinking is to enhance the eating experience. But then Jägermeister started to market itself to bartenders as a party drink rather than as something to be consumed with food. It became an instant hit in the US and elsewhere, as bartenders were looking for a trendy drink to replace tequila. Everyone seemed to like it, even though its flavor doesn't make it an obvious crowd-pleaser, and it became a long-lasting trend.

Jägermeister is a liqueur that was originally a classic digestif, that is, it was meant to be consumed after a heavy meal to help with digestion. It is made out of 56 types of herbs, roots, spices, and berries (including anise, ginger, cinnamon and juniper). Some of these ingredients are distilled, and others are infused into the alcohol as extracts. Its alcohol concentration is 35%, and it is aged for an entire year in oak barrels. Its color is very dark.

The name "Jägermeister" comes from a legend about a simple German man named Hubertus, who, in the 7th century, fought a duel to win a princess' hand in marriage. Hubertus won, married the princess, and lived with her happily ever after until she took ill and died. The lonely man left the palace, gave away all his possessions, and went into seclusion in a cabin at the heart of a desolate forest. According to an alternative version, Hubertus was himself the son of a duke, and his wife died while giving birth to their son. Either way, he dropped out of society and went to be alone in the forest, and lived mainly off what he could hunt.

One day, on one of his many hunting trips, Hubertus noticed from a distance a large and impressive stag, and prepared to shoot it. But when he looked closer he saw something incredible: A large, glowing cross hung between the stag's antlers. Hubertus had a religious epiphany. The story spread very quickly, and the young Hubertus was recognized as a saint. Because of the nature of his epiphany he became the patron saint of hunters.

In 1878, a family by the name of Mast established a distillery for a new beverage it had invented, and it decided to name it after Saint Jägermeister—"the master of hunters." The image of the stag with the cross between its antlers is the Jägermeister logo.

Hubertus, "the master of hunters", engraving, year unknown

In many countries, including the US, Jägermeister is identified with night life, parties, festivals, and good music. You probably won't be able to find a single bar that doesn't have a bottle of the beverage in the freezer. In Germany, the birthplace of Jägermeister, the beverage is not refrigerated or kept in the freezer the way it is in the US. Rather, it is served at room temperature in a lowball glass with ice.

The popular way of drinking Jägermeister: ice cold (straight from the freezer), in a shot glass or chaser. You can also drink it alongside a beer or with an energy drink, orange juice, Coke, ginger ale, or tonic water with lemon, and you can mix it into cocktails. The bonus is that Jäger will always work as a great digestif, and a shot of it will soothe the stomach after a meal.

Surfer on Acid

We're not really sure how the Surfer on Acid got its name, but you can imagine the craziness that might have led up to it. This is a very popular drink among Jägermeister fans. Its components are simple, and it's easy to make. You can serve it however you prefer: in a lowball glass without ice, or in a highball glass with ice. It's a tropical summer drink, which gets its bite from Jägermeister.

What you need
(for one highball glass)

40 ml Jägermeister
40 ml Malibu (coconut rum)
40 ml pineapple juice
Ice

What to do

Fill the glass with ice. Combine all the ingredients in a shaker with ice and shake. Strain the cocktail into the glass.

Jägermeister: A Serving Suggestion

The producers of Jägermeister recommend drinking the beverage with tonic water or with ginger beer. I also think that's the best way of drinking it.

What you need
(for one highball glass)

60 ml Jägermeister
Ginger beer or ginger ale
Ice
Slice of lime or a wedge of lemon
    for garnish

What to do

Pour the Jägermeister into the glass with ice. Add the ginger beer or ginger ale up to the lip of the glass. Garnish with the lemon or lime.

"To alcohol!
The cause of,
and solution to,
all of life's problems."

Homer Simpson

TOOTHLESS MICK

This story was told to me by my friend and colleague Lior Hargil, the man behind Tel Aviv's legendary bar the Minzar ("Monastery"). He told me about Mick, one of the funniest Irishmen ever to visit the Minzar, and he explained why you don't want an Irish smile in your Murphy's.

"How about another from my hometown?"
"Sure, Mick, here's a pint of Murphy's."
"Cheers."
"Cheers."
"Do you know I'm from Cork?"
"Yes, Mick, I know."
"And that Murphy's is from there and not from Dublin."
"Yes, Mick, I know."
"Cheers."

This conversation took place in the Minzar, sometime in the middle of the year 2000. Mick, a backpacker from Ireland, was feeling emotional about the fact that Israel had just begun to import Murphy's, the beer of his hometown. Like many other backpackers around that time, Mick hadn't done much backpacking after arriving in Israel, and instead spent most of his days in Tel Aviv, with its beaches, its clubs, and its beautiful people. Mick had been hanging around the Kerem Ha-Teimanim neighborhood of Tel Aviv for about three years, and because his tourist visa had expired in 1998, he'd decided not to leave and to support himself doing odd jobs, just to pay for his room at the hostel, and of course, to pay the Minzar. He took the Murphy's thing very seriously, and was probably the top Murphy's drinker at the pub (and competition was stiff in those days).

On one of the days that stretched into night, Mick had drunk too much again and was completely wasted. What was impressive was that he'd gotten to that point almost without drinking any whiskey. For Mick, like many others who came from the British Isles, the lack of a bell to announce last call and the fact that the place was open around the clock created serious malfunctions in his capacity to keep track of time and the amount he was drinking. That night was no different, but the final result was certainly a departure from the norm: When he was done drinking, Mick stumbled onto Allenby street and got hit by a bus.

At this point you might be thinking that this story is a tragedy, but fortunately, the mysterious phenomenon known as the luck of the Irish came into effect. The initial impact sent Mick flying unconscious into the road, and the bus just passed over him without touching him. Mick was rushed to the hospital, and an examination determined that he was almost completely unharmed—except for the fact that most of his teeth were gone. Now he looked like an extreme version of Shane MacGowan, the lead singer of the Pogues.

Though Mick was fairly clueless about such things, some of the regulars at the Minzar referred him to a lawyer who helped him sue the bus company. For a long time they would talk about the ridiculous sums of money that Mick would certainly win; the more they drank, the higher and more ridiculous those sums became. It's possible that seven-figure compensation could have been realistic, but then the Second Intifada broke out and the tourism industry imploded. Mick, who by that point had already gotten false teeth, just wanted to leave Israel as quickly as possible, so he settled for the sum of 200 thousand shekels (about 50 thousand dollars at the time). In honor of his departure and his newfound riches, he hosted a celebration at the pub, in which he treated everyone to drinks. Then, he left Israel to travel the world.

About five years later, Mick came back to visit. Of course, we caught up over a few pints of Murphy's (Facebook didn't exist yet), and Mick told me some funny stories. One of my favorites was the story of his return to Cork. After a few years of traveling, he started to run out of money, and a visit to Cork seemed like a good idea. After he got settled in, he immediately popped down to his old local pub to meet some old friends—both human friends and beer friends. After a few rounds Mick thought it would be a great idea to slip his false teeth into the Murphy's of the guy sitting next to him, "so he could see my Irish smile in his Murphy's," as Mick put it.

Unfortunately for everyone there, and especially unfortunately for him, the guy noticed the teeth smiling up at him from the glass only after he'd taken a large gulp of beer. A quick glance at Mick, flashing his toothless grin, revealed the identity of the prankster, and in a rage he threw his glass in Mick's face. Mick was ready for it and ducked, and the glass shattered in someone else's face, who, of course, got up to take revenge. Within seconds there was a full-on brawl with punching, kicking, head-butting, glass- and chair-throwing, and all the while the bartender and the owner were trying, and failing, to calm everyone down.

"And you, Mick, what did you do?"
"Me?" he smiled. "I was down on all fours, looking for my teeth."

BLUES FOR THE BOYS IN BLUE

At the beginning of one especially quiet evening, there were three people sitting at the bar. One very young man, who had just completed his compulsory military service; a much older man, old enough to forget that he'd ever served in the military; and two seats away a woman who had no relation to the military and who had a lot of experience with civilian life. The pub was pretty quiet that evening; everyone was focused on their drinks and on their own thoughts, and I kept myself busy behind the bar and didn't bother them.

Suddenly the door opened, and a police officer in uniform was standing at the door. All eyes turned to him. *What have we done now?* was the first question that popped into my mind. The second question that I asked myself was what an on-duty officer was doing at a pub. But it turned out that I was wrongfully suspicious; the officer only asked for an espresso. Within moments he paid and went on his way.

Judging from the expressions on their faces, the other three people at the bar had been having similar thoughts to mine, and when the policeman left, there was an almost audible sigh of relief. "Cops, huh?" I broke the silence. "They work so hard, and in the end instead of appreciating them, we get scared when we see them and even dislike them. What a thankless job."

The younger guy in the group smiled wanly. "It reminds me of something crazy that happened to me a few weeks ago," he began. "I have to admit that I'm not a very good driver. I usually drive too fast and don't always follow traffic laws. So I was driving through the city, and suddenly I realized that I was going in the wrong direction. I looked and saw that there weren't any cars close behind me, so I just cut across the lanes and turned around. About two seconds later, I heard the siren of a police car behind me. Unlucky me, I got pulled over. 'What did I do, Officer?' I played dumb. He asked me to get out of the car and told me that

I'd made a dangerous turn, and that I had also run a red light when making the illegal turn, and that I'd crossed over a solid white line. 'I'm going to take you off the road,' the man of the law informed me, 'and write you a big fat ticket with a court summons.' At that moment, I got out of the car, took the keys, put them in the policeman's hand and started walking away. 'What are you doing?' he asked. 'You took me off the road,' I answered. 'Take the keys, take the car, it's yours. My dad will kill me when I get home anyway; my life is over.' My misery must have been very convincing, because at that point the policeman turned to me like a kind and understanding father and said, 'OK, I'll let you go this time; I think you learned your lesson. Take the keys, drive safely and carefully, and if I ever catch you again, I'm suspending your license.'"

"That really was nice of him," I said. "You've got more luck than brains." The guy went back to his drink, and then the other guy at the bar woke up. "Speaking of nice stories about cops, I have one too," he said. "About a week ago I was driving home from the pub. Do you remember what I drank last week?" I didn't even have to think about it. "Of course, nine-and-a-half beers," I answered. "And even though I asked you to, you wouldn't leave your car here and take a cab. I wasn't sure I'd ever see you again." And he continued, "So I was driving home, or, actually zigzagging, trying to navigate through the quiet streets. I think I even drove up on the curb. Within a few minutes, a police car pulled me over. The two cops inside it turned to me: 'What happened? Are you ill?' 'No,' I answered in a moment of honesty, 'I just left the pub, I'm not used to drinking, and I feel really sick.' My honesty must have touched the hearts of these officers of the law, and one of them said kindly, 'Come, get in the police car. I'll take you home, and my friend will drive behind us in your car and park it by your house.' I was so shocked that I said nothing. When we got home I thanked the officers from all my heart and I promised I would never drink again, especially not if I was planning on driving." He finished his story while finishing his fourth beer. Another one with more luck than brains, I thought.

And then the woman began to speak; she had a story too. "Last night we went out, me and my husband and another couple of good friends of ours. We went to a pub in another town and we drank a lot. One of us, our friend, made sure not to drink too much because he was the designated driver. So far so good, right?" she asked. We all nodded and waited for her to continue. "Well, the night was over and we stumbled out to our car. Our friend, who happens to be my husband's subordinate at work, sat down at the wheel, my darling husband sat next to him, and we, the girls, plunked down in the back seat and dozed off, drunk. The driver started the car and began driving, and my drunk husband was acting like a little kid showing off his car: 'Drive faster, this car doesn't know how to drive slow. Look how responsive it is, press harder on the gas.' The driver, a responsible guy, tried to calm him down: 'Nah, I usually don't drive too fast. Go to sleep, trust me.' But my husband was the boss, after all, and he started pressuring him: 'Come on, you'll love it. This car is incredible, you won't believe what it can do.' At some point the driver started to crack, with my husband being the boss and all, and he decided to speed up. More egging on from my husband and a little more pressure on the gas pedal, and suddenly we were going 160 km per hour. And then we heard the siren... police!

"The driver stopped, I barely managed to wake up, and out of my half-sleep I heard the officer ask: 'Do you have any idea how fast you were going?' The driver apologized, stuttering, 'It was really a one-time thing, I never go above the speed limit.' The officer, of course, didn't believe him, saw the guy next to him grinning and swaying and the two women passed out in the back, and drew his conclusions. Then he turned to me: 'Ma'am, please open the window.' I opened the window, and the motion made me terribly nauseous. I knew that if I opened my mouth to speak to him, the entire contents of my stomach would spew out onto his crisp uniform. And then he looked me straight in the eye and asked: 'How can you drive with these two drunks? Don't you value your life?'"

DRINKING:
A BEGINNER'S GUIDE

THE BEGINNING OF A BEAUTIFUL FRIENDSHIP

In the movie *Leaving Las Vegas*, Nicolas Cage gives one of the most impressive performances of his career, in the role of an alcoholic who has destroyed his own life and is aware of his terminal, irreversible condition. A compulsive yearning for alcohol—a physical and emotional addiction—dictates his every move. Cage looks pale throughout most of the movie; he sweats profusely, his entire body shuddering with pain. It's a must-see for anyone who drinks alcohol or deals with it on any level.

In recent years, modern medicine has given us the green light to drink one or two glasses of alcohol per day. In fact, studies have shown that drinking one or two glasses of wine can reduce the amount of "bad" cholesterol in the body and help prevent clogged arteries and other ailments. But no one talks much about where to draw the line. Consistently drinking to excess can cause addiction just as serious as addiction to hard drugs. Alcoholism is a disease, and the recovery process is as long and difficult as they come.

In contrast to other drugs, which enter our bodies through the respiratory system or the circulatory system, alcohol enters the body through the digestive system and is absorbed in the blood through the stomach, and only then does it reach the brain. Because its journey to the brain is so prolonged, it takes at least 15 minutes after drinking alcohol to feel its effects. And it takes a long time to metabolize alcohol: The liver processes alcohol at a rate of about seven grams per hour, meaning that it takes more than three hours to metabolize a single serving of an alcoholic beverage (a shot of vodka, a glass of wine, or a pint of beer), and that's after we've lost about 10% of the alcohol through the body's natural excretions. When we're drunk we experience various temporary malfunctions in the brain—slow responses to stimuli, poor judgment, blurred vision, and failure to perform basic motor functions, frequent urination, a decrease in body temperature, and irritation of the lining of the stomach, to the point of needing to vomit.

At the same time, when consumed in moderation, alcohol can make us feel content, confident, and openhearted, and it can make us smile more. To turn alcohol into a friend rather than an enemy, and to feel healthy and good, it's important to drink responsibly, and there are rules for how to do so.

HOW TO DRINK: THE RULES

Different people react to alcohol in different ways. Various factors such as body weight, sex, an empty stomach, the components of recent meals, typical drinking habits, and experience are all crucial in determining how a person will respond to a few drinks. Alcohol is an organic toxin, which combines with additional toxins, such as the chemicals in the wooden barrel in which the drink was aged, food coloring, and material against freezing, and our bodies fight them all together.

Don't mix different types of drinks so as not to introduce too many types of toxins. The better the quality of a beverage, the fewer toxins it is likely to contain, but there are some exceptions; for example, beverages that have been aged for a long time tend to contain toxins from the wood and from the aging process. Filtered beverages that are not aged in wooden barrels (young wine, high-quality vodka, and beer are some of the main ones) contain fewer toxins. By the way, the colder a beverage is, the longer it will take it to be absorbed in the stomach.

Drink slowly and take breaks between drinks. It takes 15–20 minutes to feel the influence of a serving of alcohol, and the effects take a long time to dissipate. So there's really no point in chugging your beverages at the beginning of the evening and then complaining that you "can't feel a thing".

Make sure to **drink a lot of water while drinking alcohol**. The body uses up water molecules to metabolize alcohol, so there's a risk of becoming

"When I read about the
evils of drinking,
I gave up reading."

Henny Youngman,
American comedian and violinist

dehydrated while you drink, and you need to replenish water. Intoxication is similar to dehydration: it causes headaches, nausea, etc. Women have lower concentrations than men do of the enzyme that metabolizes alcohol, which is why women who are not used to drinking tend to get drunk more quickly than men.

"Line" your stomach with solid food that can absorb alcohol. It helps to eat food that is high in fat, because the fat does not dissolve in water and it slows down the rate of alcohol absorption, so it takes longer for the alcohol to go to your head.

If, in spite of everything, you've gotten drunk, it's a good idea to drink a large bottle of water before bed to prevent dehydration. If you forget to hydrate and wake up in the morning with a hangover, you should drink water or fruit juice. A light meal will help the remaining alcohol be absorbed. Avoid coffee and tea, which are diuretics.

When consumed in moderation, alcohol can make you feel great, physically and emotionally. Social drinking is fun and brings people together, makes us friendlier, and somehow deepens the laugh lines at the corners of our mouths. Winston Churchill is quoted as saying, "I have taken more out of alcohol than it has taken out of me", and with good reason. Most importantly, when you drink to your health, you should take that sentiment seriously: Never drink and drive.

THE HOME BAR

Many older movies feature scenes in which a man comes home after a long day at work and the little wife, who was waiting for him at home all day, rushes to greet him with a glass of whisky. In today's movies, the wives aren't little anymore, and they don't rush to greet their husbands anymore.

The man pours himself a drink, and the woman, who's also just come home from work, joins him.

In Ireland the guy coming back from work takes his entire family to the neighborhood pub. The kids play there together while Mom and Dad drink their beer. The English leave work and hit the pub before going home, thirstily gulping the pint they've been waiting for all day. And later in the evening, sophisticated young drinkers go out to cocktail bars to sample stylish new drinks.

In Israel, there's no real drinking culture; it's still developing. People go out to the pub mainly to meet friends, to hang out and to eat. But what do you do when friends come over, and you want to serve them something a little more interesting than a glass of wine? For these scenarios, it's a good idea to invest in a well-stocked home bar.

You should treat your home bar like a lab for producing beverages. The equipment must be professional, functional, and easy to operate. Not all the tools have to be top-of-the-line; you can improvise some using other implements that are available around the house, but you should at least make sure to have the basics.

EQUIPMENT

GLASSES

It's a good idea to have several different types of glasses in your home bar, including highball glasses, lowball or Old Fashioned glasses (also called whisky glasses or rocks glasses), cocktail (martini) glasses, which are stemmed glasses with an inverted cone-shaped bowl, shot glasses or chasers, brandy snifters, and wine glasses.

White Wine Glass

Red Wine Glass

Cocktail Glass

Champagne Flute

Armagnac Glass

Old Fashioned /
Lowball Glass

Highball Glass

Collins Glass

Irish Coffee Mug

Punch Cup

Port Glass

Sherry Glass

Cordial Glass

Margarita Glass

Cognac Balloon
Snifter

Beer Mug

Beer Glass

Vodka Shot Glass

Shot Glass

LIQUOR

Stock your home bar with high-quality labels to prevent headaches, nausea and other problems related to mediocre alcohol. You don't have to buy the most expensive beverages; you can find decent affordable alcohol at most liquor stores or at the Duty Free shop. The basic drinks you should keep on hand are vodka, gin, light rum and dark rum, tequila, whisky (different types), good brandy (preferably Cognac), aperitifs (like vermouth, Campari, and anise-based beverages), herbaceous digestifs or liqueurs based on whatever you like, wine, beer and soft drinks, and of course, anything else you enjoy.

COCKTAIL MIXERS

Mixology offers a lot of opportunities to be creative. You can add all types of ingredients from your home kitchen, according to your personal preference. But there are a few basic ingredients that no home bar should be without:

Angostura bitters. An alcoholic mixture that serves as a spice to add a bitter and aromatic flavor to cocktails. A critical ingredient in some cocktails.

Lemon (or lime) juice and sugar. You can buy pre-made lemon/lime syrup or mix it up yourself (three parts lemon or lime to one part sugar).

Fruit juices and fresh fruit.

Additional soft drinks, including soda water, tonic water, ginger ale, bitter lemon.

And last but not least—**ice and lemons**.

Can and bottle openers

Wine corkscrew (a "waiter's corkscrew"
is the best and most efficient),
beer bottle openers and can openers

Shaker

Used to shake, mix and chill
cocktails with ice

Jigger

A measuring tool used for liquids.
Alternatively, you can use a shot
glass, which contains 60 ml.

Blender that crushes ice

If you don't have one, you can use
a meat mallet and a clean towel.

Pourer

Placed on the mouth of a bottle to pour
liquid into glasses in a controlled way.

Ice bucket

Should be insulated to keep in the
cold. Typically has a double wall
made of plastic.

Stirrers

Used to stir drinks and to
decorate glasses

Coasters

A coaster is placed under the glass to
prevent it from sweating on the table

Everything else is just standard
equipment available in any home:
a cutting board, knives, a long spoon,
strainer, a juicer, and more.

ACKNOWLEDGEMENTS

There are so many people to thank, and it's hard and even impossible to include every person who contributed to this book in some way. So thanks to everyone I met along the way and who told me a story that got etched in my memory. Thanks to all the alcohol producers, the distillers and the bartenders I met and who made me fall in love again and again with this fascinating world. Many, many thanks to the alcohol companies that believed in the book and supported it: IBBL Spirits and Asaf Ivanir, Asaf Mor and Dudi Zats; to the Hacarem company and Ronit Avner and Gal Yaniv; and to the Tempo company and Tamar Cohen. Thank you to the bar owners who gladly participated in the process of creating this book: Mosh Budnik and the Social Club, Ariel Leizgold, the Bell Boy and 223, Bar Shira and the Imperial, Shmulik Wohlberg and the Cerveceria, who created delicious and stunningly beautiful cocktails, and patiently allowed them to be photographed, and to other bars where we took our gorgeous atmosphere pictures: Wine Bar (Brut), Rothschild 12, Hotel Montefiore, and Hide & Seek. Thanks to everyone involved in the publication process: to LunchBox, who believed in the book and treated every detail with such care. Thanks to Ofer Vardi and Michal Rymon Marom, without whom this book would never have existed; to the amazing and supportive Zohara Ron, who was able to comb patiently through the stories and to get the best out of them; to Galit and Bosmat, who checked every comma; to Keren & Golan for their amazing graphic design; to Michal Revivo for her incredible photography; and to Galia Ornan for styling the photo shoots just so. Thanks to Karen Marron, for her excellent and precise translation, and for her efforts to adapt every detail of this book to suit an English-speaking audience.

And special thanks to my beloved partner and children, for your support, your understanding, your empathy and your boundless love. Giving birth to this book was an amazing, enjoyable and unforgettable experience.

Mira Eitan

"Young Sick Bacchus" (detail), painting by Caravaggio, c. 1592